KATHI LIPP & CHERI GREGORY

HARVEST HOUSE PUBLISHERS
EUGENE, OREGON

Published in association with Books & Such Literary Management, 52 Mission Circle, Suite 122, PMB 170, Santa Rosa, CA 95409–5370, www.booksandsuch.com.

And in association with the Steve Laube Agency, LLC, 24 W. Camelback Rd. A635, Phoenix, Arizona 85013.

Cover and interior design by Studio Gearbox
Cover photo © ozzichk, Leria Katerina, Mara Fribus, Beliavskii Igor /Shutterstock

For bulk, special sales, or ministry purchases, please call 1 (800) 547-8979.
Email: Customerservice@hhpbooks.com

M is a federally registered trademark of the Hawkins Children's LLC. Harvest House Publishers, Inc., is the exclusive licensee of the trademark.

An Abundant Place
Copyright © 2022 by Kathi Lipp and Cheri Gregory
Published by Harvest House Publishers
Eugene, Oregon 97408
www.harvesthousepublishers.com

ISBN 978-0-7369-7643-5 (hardcover)
ISBN 978-0-7369-7644-2 (eBook)

Library of Congress Control Number: 2021943918

Printed in the United States of America

21 22 23 24 25 26 27 28 29 /VP/ 10 9 8 7 6 5 4 3 2 1

Contents

An Invitation... 5

✓ Crafting a Space: Preparing for Your Time with God 9

✓ Creating Space: Your Deeper Dive into Scripture........... 13

✔ Power Outage Plan..............17

Inviting the Holy into
My Humble 23

Overgrown Tomato
Plants 31

The World as Worship........ 39

Reminders of War,
Promise of Peace........... 45

✔ Choose Your Own
Adventure.......................... 51

Neither Slumber
nor Sleep............................ 59

DIY... 65

Strengthening Through
Stretching..........................71

Working It Out......................77

Kikuyu Grass......................... 85

✓ Pain in the Neck 93

Purr-fect Trust..................... 101

A Life Built on
Gratitude 107

Fruit in Season..................... 113

One Egg Too Far.................119

Corrosion 125

Chopping Wood 131

For Freedom........................ 137

Not Hard Enough...............143

Motion and Direction...... 149

Fire Starting 155

Stay in the Water..............163

Power, Love, and
Self-Discipline 171

Tide Tables 179

How Does Your
Garden Grow?.................185

A New Normal 193

Checking Myself into
the Greenhouse 201

Right Where You Are
Right Now........................209

Hope in a Seed
Catalog 215

An Invitation

KATHI

For someone who doesn't believe in luck, I feel like the luckiest woman in the world.

I've spent the majority of my life living in San Jose, California—the heart of Silicon Valley—in tiny townhouses with no perceptible land, just a tiny cement patio for a backyard, and neighbors the width of a wall away. I longed daily to get off our busy street and head somewhere, anywhere, to get away from the crowding, the noise, and let's be honest, every once in a while, my kids.

I would pack up my laptop, some books, and my Bible. One of the advantages of living in the Bay Area was that no matter whether you headed east or west, something wonderful (mountains or beach) was just a couple of hours away. Sometimes with my husband, sometimes with friends, and when I was on a deadline, sometimes by myself. I would hole up in a tiny cabin on my own or in a big beach house with friends to read, talk, write, and just get away to be with people I love and to spend time with God.

After spending more than I could reasonably afford on short getaways to retreat centers and Airbnbs, my husband and I finally made the life-changing decision to move to the mountains of Northern California.

We were just looking for a cabin in the woods that we could stay in when we wanted to and rent out the rest of the time to cover the mortgage. What we ended up doing was buying a house on 33 acres in the middle of Northern California among the rolling hills of stunning wineries, where we now live with our dog, our cat, four chickens, and occasionally, a black bear who likes to see if he can break into our garage for snacks.

So now, the place where people dream of getting away? It's my full-time residence.

Cheri, on the other hand, has spent the last fifteen years in paradise.

Cheri is one of the relatively few people who actually live on the Pacific coast. Her backyard is the ocean. Cheri lives at the boarding school where she and her husband teach. What was once a military base on the beach now houses not only Cheri and her family, but an assortment of teachers, staff, and students from all over the country and around the world.

Both Cheri and I, almost by accident, live in places people dream about visiting. And now, we want to share those places with you.

There were many years—because of time, money, kids, and responsibilities—that the word *retreat* was not in our vocabulary. There were days when I wanted to get away from the noise and chaos so much that I would "retreat" to my minivan in the garage. (My trick was to tell any kid who came out to ask me a question that we needed to clean the car out together. That limited the number of van visitors I had to contend with.)

And that may be where you are in life right this minute. If you are in the place where the word *retreat* feels like it is only a far-off fantasy, Cheri and I have an invitation for you. Come join us.

If you came to the beach, Cheri would tuck you into one of the guest rooms on the campus where she lives. She would arrange a little basket with a few teas, a cozy blanket, and then point you in the direction of the beach for when you wanted to take your walk.

And if you were coming to the mountains? I would show you the sunniest spot on our deck, or give you the reclining chair near the fire—depending on what time of year you were here. I would show you where the coffee was and warn you about chickens who like to look over your shoulder when you're reading the Gospel of John.

But since you can't get away, please, let us, in the pages that follow, bring the mountain and the beach to you.

In the Seventh Day Adventist tradition, nature is often referred to as "God's second book." I'm not a Seventh Day Adventist, but I have come to discover that nature, besides God's Word, has become my greatest teacher. And why am I surprised? So much of what is recorded in the Bible is tying God to nature.

The way God has ordered and ordained life outside my four walls has made me understand and be mystified by God so much more than I have by any other teacher in my life. From the rhythm of the mountain to the schedule of our chickens, I see God's design over every inch of our land.

We know that not everyone has the opportunity to spend as much time in nature as the two of us do. But it is our hope that through these observations and devotions, you will be excited and intrigued to view God through the lens of the nature around you: the trees at your neighborhood park, the dog lying next to you on the couch (like mine is right now as I write this), or the tomato plant growing on your back step that you hope to turn into a caprese salad—someday.

God keeps unfolding His truths all around us. It's our prayer that each of us would make the space to see, hear, taste, smell, and feel those truths for ourselves.

Welcome to your retreat.

Crafting a Space

Preparing for Your Time with God

KATHI

There is just something about a retreat, isn't there? A time and a space set aside just for you.

I've spent a good portion of my life being a part of creating places of retreat for other women. Whether it's been hosting writers and friends at our mountain retreat in Northern California, or leading women in prayer on the beaches of the Pacific, the place, while a lovely backdrop, was never the focus. The focus has always been creating a space without worldly distractions—a space to really and truly encounter God. A space to usher in the holy squeezed in between the midst of the everyday. What the setting does is offer us a chance to quiet our hearts and minds. The opportunity is presented. We get to choose whether we take it or not.

And that is what Cheri and I are offering to do here—inviting you into a spacious place. Giving you the opportunity to quiet your heart and mind.

There is an intentionality to creating a spacious place no

matter where you are. So we thought it best to share our space with you—but also our means of not getting overwhelmed by the world and its distractions. We want you too to have the opportunity to leave some of the world behind and come into the same spacious place we enjoy every day. No matter where you are or what area you live in, we are all afforded the opportunity to create a spacious place for ourselves.

Here's how to get started.

Create an actual space. My space depends on what time of year it is. When I lived in Silicon Valley, I would spend late spring through early fall on our postage stamp-sized back patio. I had a chair back there with a table just big enough for my Bible, a book, and a cup of coffee (because, what else do you really need?). In the colder months, I had a corner of the couch that was all mine. A comfy place to sit and be was all I needed.

Nowadays, I spend the warm months on a chair by the chicken coop, and colder months on our living room couch by the wood burning stove.

You may be more comfortable at a table (especially if you love to journal or draw). Just make sure it's a place you feel comfortable and snug in and look forward to going to.

Have your supplies. I would recommend a couple of items to make your time as retreat-like as possible without leaving your house:

- A blanket. I like to have a blanket on me when I'm

spending time with God. There is just something so satisfying about being curled up when I am meditating.

- Your beverage of choice. I know it's possible to meet with God without coffee, but I'm not here to prove that theory. I've heard that tea can work as well, but I would have no personal experience with that approach. If I'm meeting God later in the day, iced tea can work in a pinch. There is just something so lovely about preparing yourself a cuppa. There is an intentionality to the preparation—as if you were preparing to sit down with an old friend for a long talk.
- A notebook. Yes, we want you to write in this book. But here's my hope: that God will reveal more to you than can be contained in these pages. That is where the notebook comes in.
- Your favorite pen. I happen to be an InkJoy girl myself, but whatever pen thrills your heart when you touch it to paper, make sure that is in your arsenal.
- Your Bible. My hope is that you will, some days, want to go deeper into what you've read. That you'll want to read the bits before and after the featured verse.

If this seems like too much, skip what doesn't work for you. But here is what I've found: The more ritual I have around my time with God, the easier it is for me to enter into God's presence when I really, really don't feel as if I have the time, the energy, or let's be honest, the desire. Ritual can bring us into a spacious place so much more quickly than when we just let things happen. So grab your cuppa and snuggle in. We're so glad you're here.

Creating Space

Your Deeper Dive into Scripture

KATHI

While you're here on retreat with us, we want to give you the space to go deeper into Scripture. After each devotion, I want to take you through a guided meditation on the Scripture we are focusing on. We'll be using the word SPACE as our guide.

Speak
Ponder
Act
Commit
Express

Speak

Yes, I want you to audibly (out loud) speak the focus Scripture. And I am going to up it: I want you to speak it out loud three times.

Why out loud? And why three times?

Glad you asked. When we read anything quietly to ourselves,

it's easy to get it over with. It's so easy to miss key words, or the turn of a phrase. But reading aloud, and reading it intentionally to not miss a word? You will internalize the verse so much more deeply than just skimming it to get it done.

God meets me with spoken Scripture in a different way than if I read it quietly to myself. It may feel silly at first, reading something aloud to just yourself, but soon, you will discover the power in reading Scripture with your voice—even if in an empty room.

So what if you're in a room with six other people while you're doing this devotion, and reading Scripture aloud would not just be awkward, but would interfere with your daughter's Zoom call for school?

No worries. I have something I like to call reading silently aloud. This is when I silently read the Scripture but focus on each word with intention—as if I were speaking the Scripture, but only in my head. Try it. You read differently when you read to speak—if only to yourself.

Ponder

After you've read the Scripture passage three times aloud, take a few moments to just sit quietly and let the words flow over you.

When I think of pondering God's Word, I think about the verse and its meaning—why is God bringing this verse to me now? How does this verse stir me as a child of God?

We have a beautiful example of this in the Gospel of Luke:

"Mary treasured up all these things and pondered them in her heart" (2:19). Mary didn't share the revelation right away. She sat quietly with it and treasured it.

I'm someone who, when reading a piece of Scripture in a new way for the first time, loves to share right away what I've learned. But sometimes, it's not for us to share. It's for us to treasure. And in that quiet meditation, questions may arise.

If they do, write them down. You may want to do a deeper study of the passage or go and read the whole chapter. Or maybe today is the day to just sit with that one verse and ask God to reveal more to you on those few words.

Act

When I'm reading a verse, I often ask myself, "Is there something God wants me to do because of reading this verse today?" Look for the application in the verses that say, "Go do this," or "Think on this." What is the action God is asking you to take in this verse?

Commit

God wrote Scripture to reveal Himself to us, His children. In Scripture lies God's promises to us about who He is and what He promises to us. Look for that in the daily passage. Does He promise to sustain you? Love you? Be with you? Look for the promise and write it down here.

Express

Finally, take a moment to express to God how you think and feel about your time wrestling with that piece of Scripture. Did you feel loved, cherished, or cared for? Or maybe challenged, confronted, or even convicted? It's amazing what feelings and thoughts come up when you have a heart that has created space.

Power Outage Plan

CHERI

I will say of the LORD, "He is my refuge and
my fortress, my God, in whom I trust."

PSALM 91:2

Our first power outage was so . . . romantic.

We lit candles, bundled up in blankets, crowded together on the couch, and reminisced about our favorite family vacations. At some point, Daniel pulled out his guitar and sat by the fireplace, and we harmonized to old hymns. When the lights sprang back on, I longed to turn them back off so we could linger in the "Kum Ba Yah" moment.

Flash forward 15 years later, to 7:43 a.m. on the second Tuesday of a new year. One moment I was answering email, and the next I was shouting, "This canNOT be HAPPENING!" as my Wi-Fi signal disappeared and computer alarms screeched throughout the house.

At first, I hoped it was just a temporary disruption of service and I could get back to my jam-packed schedule by 8:00 a.m. Or 8:15 a.m. Or 8:30 a.m. Maybe 9:00 a.m at the latest. By 10:00, my cell phone battery was drained by my frantic—and mostly futile — attempts to learn how widespread the power outage was and when service would be restored.

It turned out that the power company had cut electricity to our entire county because high winds were creating extreme fire hazard conditions. One source suggested that the power might stay out for four days.

No.

NO.

NO!

This canNOT be happening!

I stared at my Google Calendar. On Sunday night, I'd planned out my week with such care. Everything on my schedule was vital. Everything needed to happen in the exact order I'd laid out. But there I was, about to miss a scheduled meeting, unable to notify anyone.

And then . . .

Well, I wish I could tell you, "And then, I heard the still small voice of God speaking to me, and His power was all I needed." What actually happened is that I proceeded to lose it for the rest of the day. *I can't believe I'm losing all this time! Just look at everything that isn't getting done! I planned so carefully, but now I'm falling so far behind! I'll never catch back up! This is so unfair!*

We lost power for 24 hours. And for 24 hours, I lost my sense of perspective so completely, I was exhausted for the rest of the week.

In the days after, I reached out to a few friends, explained what had happened, and asked, "How do you recover when you've lost time and have a packed schedule?"

They all responded with immediate sympathy and excellent suggestions. Then one posed a question that stopped me in my tracks. "Did it occur to you that God might have been inviting you to rest until the power came back on?"

Rest? On a workday?

No. That absolutely did not occur to me.

I thought back to how frantic I'd felt all day, how fitfully I'd slept that night. Twenty-four hours without power meant 24 hours without productivity, and I'd lost my mind trying to salvage it.

Did it occur to you that God might have been inviting you to rest until the power came back on? God would never do that to me! But my inner sarcasm fell flat as a deeper truth arose. Actually, He would. He's been inviting me to seek refuge in Him for as long as I can remember.

Ever since that day, I've been wondering: What might those 24 hours have been like if instead of flailing away in a losing battle against a reality I couldn't change, my actions had said, "He is my refuge and my fortress, my God in whom I trust"? Since I'm obviously not the kind of person who reacts well in crisis, I listed some important steps we could take in our next emergency and posted them on our fridge:

1. *Shut down* all computers.

2. *Assume* this will last longer than expected.

3. *Notify* anyone who is counting on me.

4. *Ask* myself, "What if this situation is an invitation from God to take refuge in Him?"

5. *Pray*, "Lord, what would You have me do during this unexpected blessing of time?"

Whatever recurring emergencies you face, a predetermined, printed plan can make the experience a little less stressful and infuse a much-needed element of peace. Having a step-by-step plan helps you focus on what you can do, not obsess over what you can't. And accepting God's invitation to take refuge in Him reminds you to rely on His power rather than depending on your own.

The Next, Most Faith-Filled Step

What preparations can you plan, print, and post for the recurring emergencies you experience?

_____

_____

_____

_____

_____

_____

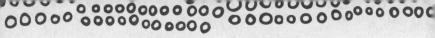

Creating Space

Speak

Read the passage aloud three times.

Ponder

Take a moment to let the words silently flow over you.

Now, some questions to ponder:

    What does the passage say?

    Why is God bringing you this passage now?

    Who comes to mind as you read this passage?

    What thoughts come to mind as you ponder?

_____

_____

_____

_____

_____

_____

_____

_____

_____

_____

_____

_____

_____

Act

Is there something God wants you to do because of reading this verse today?

_____

_____

_____

_____

Commit

What has God committed to you in this verse? What promises or truths can you make room for in your thinking?

_____

_____

_____

_____

_____

Express

Finally, take a moment to express aloud to God how you think and feel about your time making space for this piece of Scripture.

_____

_____

_____

_____

_____

Inviting the Holy into My Humble

KATHI

*In your relationships with one another, have the
same mindset as Christ Jesus: Who, being in very
nature God, did not consider equality with God something
to be used to his own advantage; rather, he made himself
nothing by taking the very nature of a servant.*

PHILIPPIANS 2:5-7

I've told my husband our whole marriage, "If you're looking for the strategic way of doing things, come to me. I'm your girl to get things done in the most efficient way possible." In other words, the laziest way of getting something done.

As a child, I would do just about anything to avoid work. This included paying my brother to do my chores; hiding dirty clothes under my bed; and one memorable time, putting dirty dishes in the oven so my mom wouldn't see them.

As an adult, I've finally figured out the only one I was hurting with my laziness was myself. Dishes that didn't get done one day were still going to be waiting for me the next day. Laundry that I let sit for days would pile up until my kids were tempted to use bandanas as underwear—or just go commando.

So as I got older, I learned the art of distraction in order to soldier on and get things done. Folding clothes wasn't so bad as long as there was an episode of *Friends* playing in the background. And cooking dinner and doing dishes weren't such a problem as long as I was in the middle of a good audiobook I could keep playing the entire time. And the treadmill? It only got treaded on when I could scroll Facebook at the same time.

And this worked, pretty much, until I got to my most dreaded of all chores—cleaning out the chicken coop. It helped a little when I told the ladies I was giving them a spa treatment and listened to soothing music while I was mucking out their roost. But for the most part, it was just cleaning up chicken poop, and there wasn't enough distraction in the world to make it tolerable.

Then came the day I left my cell phone upstairs at the house. I only had 15 minutes to clean out the coop before my next meeting. Running up to get my cell phone simply to listen to music or an audiobook would eat into about five of those minutes, and then I wouldn't be able to check off "cleaned the coop" from my list. And there's nothing worse than not being able to check something off my list.

I decided to soldier on and clean out the chicken coop with nothing playing but my own overthinking thoughts.

At first, I hated it. Ha-ted it! All I had to concentrate on was the task at hand (poop)—and what was going on in my own brain. So many of us struggle with this: having to have noise going all the time in order to drown out the thoughts we don't want to deal with. It's just easier to put on a podcast and deal with someone else's thoughts, rather than our own.

But with my mind freed up for the first time in a very long time, I was amazed. My thoughts, after creating a laundry list of to-do items, turned to the verses in Philippians I'd read earlier in the week.

While it might seem irreverent to commune with Jesus while scooping chicken poop, what I realized is this: Jesus, who started off in the most humble of circumstance—not that much different from a chicken coop—chose to be humble to love each and every one of us.

Meditating on Jesus happens in our house of worship on a Sunday, and a chicken house on a Tuesday. We just need to still our minds and focus on Him, wherever we are, whatever mess we're cleaning up, whatever we're doing.

Ever since that day, I've been increasing the amount of work I do sound- and screen-free. It's amazing what happens when the brain is given some space. When there is quiet, God uses an unlimited number of ways to speak: bringing worship songs and Bible verses to mind, talking through the wind in the trees, and revealing His thoughts through the click-click-click of the birds.

I realized I had been treating my daily quiet time with God like my workout on the treadmill: something I knew was good for me but wanted to get over with as soon as possible so I could get to the long list of everything else I needed to do that day.

But I've started to reframe that time in the morning. Instead of it being the start and finish of my "spiritual time" for the day, I'm treating it as setting the tone for the day, entering into the holy and looking at every activity throughout the day as a chance to be present in that holy. I believe God cares equally about my scheduled time with Him, the walk I take with my husband through the woods, the time I play with my dog, the time I do the dishes, and yes, the time spent cleaning out the chicken coop. He is there, whatever I'm doing.

The Next, Most Faith-Filled Step

Brother Lawrence, a monk in seventeenth-century France, was assigned to the monastery kitchen. This is where he learned the beauty in not doing great things, but doing small things with a greater love for God:

> Nor is it needful that we should have great things to do ... We can do little things for God; I turn the cake that is frying on the pan for love of him, and that done, if there is nothing else to call me, I prostrate myself in worship before him, who has given me grace to work; afterwards I rise happier than a king. It is enough

**for me to pick up but a straw from the ground
for the love of God.**

Here's the question I want you to ask yourself: What is the humblest part of your day? Is it changing diapers? Serving your boss? Running errands for your parents? Folding clothes?

Now, are there ways to invite the holy into your humble? Could you pray over your son's future while you change his diaper? Could you remember the mantra "God is with me" as you breathe out at work? Could you pray for your husband as you pair his socks?

_____

_____

_____

_____

_____

Creating Space

Speak

Read the passage aloud three times.

Ponder

Take a moment to let the words silently flow over you.

Now, some questions to ponder:

> What does the passage say?
>
> Why is God bringing you this passage now?
>
> Who comes to mind as you read this passage?
>
> What thoughts come to mind as you ponder?

_____

_____

_____

_____

_____

_____

_____

_____

_____

_____

_____

_____

_____

Act

Is there something God wants you to do because of reading this verse today?

_____

_____

_____

_____

Commit

What has God committed to you in this verse? What promises or truths can you make room for in your thinking?

_____

_____

_____

_____

_____

Express

Finally, take a moment to express aloud to God how you think and feel about your time making space for this piece of Scripture.

_____

_____

_____

_____

_____

Overgrown Tomato Plants

CHERI

Let us not become weary in doing good, for at the proper time we will reap a harvest if we do not give up.

GALATIANS 6:9

When my son Jonathon announced, "I'm going to plant a raised garden," visions of caprese salads danced in my head. My mouth watered as I imagined slices of fragrant home-grown tomatoes layered with fresh mozzarella cheese.

"Son, I am always here to support you," I said. "And eat any tomatoes you grow, of course."

As Jonathon measured, planned, and made trips to Home Depot, I worked hard to curb my urges to "help." *He's old enough to do this on his own!* I reminded myself more than once. Per day.

During the early days, Jonathon fussed over his baby plants, weeding, watering, checking for signs of disease. When a freak hailstorm flattened many of the plants, he was distraught. But his dismay turned to amazement when he discovered that although the plants initially looked destroyed, with a little TLC, they all perked right back up again.

As the days and weeks went by, Jonathon kept tending his

garden . . . albeit less frequently than at first. Again, I resisted the impulse to meddle. *It's his garden. He needs to learn by doing.*

We cheered when little yellow flowers started blooming. Soon, we were remarking in amazement at the abundance of tiny green tomatoes.

Then I left home for two weeks. When I returned, it looked like the tomato garden had gone on steroids. The vines had tripled in size, and there were hundreds of small tomatoes. The promise of a bountiful harvest delighted me. But the look of the tomato plants themselves worried me. The vines were leaning way out of the container, and the weight of the tomatoes was dragging the vines down toward the ground.

Once more, I bit my tongue. *He's not asking for my help, so I won't insert myself into his project.*

The day finally came when Jonathon announced, "I have to do something about the tomato plants. They're leaning over so far, they're going to break if I don't do something. Would you be willing to help me tie them up?"

Our first hour of staking the tomato plants was almost fun. Tracing which stems were attached to which stalks was like solving a puzzle. But as the second hour rolled around, I stepped back to survey our progress, and my heart sank.

We've hardly made a dent. This is a complete disaster.

I wiped sweat from my forehead.

This is't even my problem. I should just call it quits.

I heaved a peeved sigh.

This was all entirely preventable. If only I had stepped in sooner . . .

Glancing at Jonathon, I was surprised to find his mood the opposite of mine. His expression was steady, patient, curious. Instead of chastising himself for what he had (or hadn't) done in the past, he focused on what he could do in the moment.

Once we finished, Jonathon shared what he'd learned for the future. Rather than seeing his overgrown tomato garden as a failure, he viewed it as a successful experiment that would inform his gardening practices for years to come.

Jonathon and I learned practical lessons about not becoming weary in doing good that day.

Sometimes, "doing good" is about what we don't do. I came to the valuable realization that all the times I'd bitten my tongue and decided not to meddle had truly paid off. Because I did not help until asked, Jonathon experienced the consequences of leaving the tomato plants unstaked, and he'd learned from those consequences. While I did not enjoy spending three hours in the hot sun, the whole experience felt less wearying and more rewarding when I focused on the long-term good it had done my son.

Sometimes, "doing good" is about what we'll do differently next time. Jonathon's determination to spend as much time as needed tying up the overgrown tomato plants led him to make an important decision. For his next garden, he invested in high-quality metal stakes so he could train his second round of tomato plants to grow the right way from day one.

And since we did not give up, we both reaped a harvest, "at the proper time." My harvest was immediate. It was witnessing— and learning from—my son's maturity. Although I'd initially felt critical of his allowing the tomato plants to become overgrown in the first place, I now look back on our time working side by side to tie up the vines as a special memory. His steadiness and curiosity helped me dial down on my instinctive perfectionism and simply be present "doing good" alongside him.

Jonathon's harvest, of course, came during the weeks to come. It was a bumper crop of homegrown tomatoes from plants that he'd watered, weeded, tended, tied up, and ultimately picked, all by hand.

What's making you weary right now? Feeling like you're in the midst of a tangle of overgrown tomato vines? Trust God's promises and the growth processes He's put into place.

Don't give up. Keep doing good and learning as you go. Your harvesttime is on its way.

The Next, Most Faith-Filled Step

What's the tangle of overgrown tomato vines in your life right now?

_____

_____

How is God calling you to keep doing good by *not* doing something?

_____

_____

_____

_____

_____

_____

How is God calling you to keep doing good by doing something *differently* next time?

_____

_____

_____

_____

_____

_____

When it's the proper time, what kind of harvest do you anticipate?

_____

_____

_____

_____

_____

_____

Creating Space

Speak

Read the passage aloud three times.

Ponder

Take a moment to let the words silently flow over you.

Now, some questions to ponder:

What does the passage say?

Why is God bringing you this passage now?

Who comes to mind as you read this passage?

What thoughts come to mind as you ponder?

_____

_____

_____

_____

_____

_____

_____

_____

_____

_____

_____

_____

_____

Act

Is there something God wants you to do because of reading this verse today?

_____

_____

_____

_____

Commit

What has God committed to you in this verse? What promises or truths can you make room for in your thinking?

_____

_____

_____

_____

_____

Express

Finally, take a moment to express aloud to God how you think and feel about your time making space for this piece of Scripture.

_____

_____

_____

_____

_____

the World as Worship

KATHI

Let the fields be jubilant, and everything in them;
let all the trees of the forest sing for joy.

PSALM 96:12

In the year of COVID, like so much of the world, church was shut down.

I understood why it had to happen—we were in a pandemic, after all—but I missed so much of it. The preaching and teaching, the fellowship, communion, but most of all, I missed the worship. I missed standing shoulder to shoulder with other people who love God and lifting my hands and my heart in praise. I missed that intimacy with God, even amid hundreds of other people.

So as with every other situation in 2020, it was a time to get creative. Like other believers, we worshipped from our living rooms, sitting on the couch, our dog and cat cuddled into our makeshift pew.

It was good. But it wasn't the same. And I, not knowing how to fix it, started to withdraw from worship. If it wasn't going to be how I needed it to be, I would just skip it.

And that is when I began to realize a deep truth about

myself: I was relying too much on the band and the worship pastor, the lights and the production. If something was missing from my worship, it wasn't the church, it was me. I had allowed my life to become too noisy, and to break through that noise, I needed my worship to be equally as noisy. I was relying on God and a bunch of singers on stage to get me to a place of worship. And that wasn't their job. It was mine.

That year was a time for me to get quiet and figure out what my responsibility was in my role of worshipper.

When your regular worship has been taken away, your heart longs for and seeks out new ways to worship. Taking a walk with my husband through our forest, I notice that when there is wind, not only do the trees make a delightful rustling sound, but the breeze goes through them in such a way that they actually lightly sing. I had heard the wind howl before, but I never thought of the trees singing. But that is exactly what they were doing—singing over us as we walked through the forest.

How amazing is it that God designed the trees so they would sing? And every time I hear that singing, I think to myself how God has designed things that I didn't even notice until the second half of my life. That there are still new ways to worship God even when my traditional, easy, expected ways have been stripped from me. The methods may change, but the purpose stays the same—to worship God.

And the worship doesn't stop with my ears. As we drive

these roads around our mountain, we are surrounded by over forty wineries in our area. I have, until this time in my life, only had one vision of what wineries look like: great green plants heavy-laden with purple and white grapes. Just like every movie I've ever seen. But with our weekly trips to and from town, sitting in the passenger seat, I have had ample time to notice the changing seasons of the vineyards.

We started our drives through the mountains in the winter when the fields and vineyards are at their bleakest. Everything on the vine has died, the grass is brown, and the best thing about the drive is not the sights, but the smells of the farmers, vintners, and landowners creating heaping burn piles to clear the fields (which, by the way, is one of the top three smells ever, competing with fresh coffee and Krispy Kreme donuts when the fresh sign is on).

But wait through all the seasons, and you get to fall. And fall on the mountain is a worship experience all its own. It is impossible to look at the vineyards and the fields and not want to thank God that you get to be a human, living on this planet, who gets to see, up close and personal, the miracle that is the riotous colors of the fields.

Is it worship for a grape to go through a life cycle? I guess if the rocks can cry out, a grape, living its life, can also be worship. But my noticing and thanking God for the life cycle of that grape? That is, indeed, worship.

As I write this, we are still not meeting as a church body, in person. But we will, someday soon. And I will rejoice. But I will also be, in a way, guarding my worship when I get back to the church building. I will celebrate getting to see the people I love, but I will no longer rely on them to be the bridge to the One whom I love. That is not their job; it is not their burden. That is too much to entrust another human with.

God has given me an abundance of opportunities to worship Him. I just need to quiet the noise and pay attention to what He has already provided.

The Next, Most Faith-Filled Step

The older I get, the more I see that God is using more than His Word and His people to connect with me. He is using the trees, my chickens, the fields, and the flowers.

Take one full minute and study something in nature. The tree outside your window. The plant on your back porch. The dog lying next to you on the couch. What does God want to say to you through them?

_____

_____

_____

_____

_____

_____

_____

Creating Space

Speak

Read the passage aloud three times.

Ponder

Take a moment to let the words silently flow over you.

Now, some questions to ponder:

What does the passage say?

Why is God bringing you this passage now?

Who comes to mind as you read this passage?

What thoughts come to mind as you ponder?

_____

_____

_____

_____

_____

_____

_____

_____

_____

_____

_____

_____

_____

_____

Act

Is there something God wants you to do because of reading this verse today?

_____

_____

_____

_____

Commit

What has God committed to you in this verse? What promises or truths can you make room for in your thinking?

_____

_____

_____

_____

_____

Express

Finally, take a moment, to express aloud to God how you think and feel about your time making space for this piece of Scripture.

_____

_____

_____

_____

_____

Reminders of War, Promise of Peace

CHERI

I have told you these things, so that in me you may
have peace. In this world you will have trouble.
But take heart! I have overcome the world.

JOHN 16:33

When we first moved to the Monterey Bay Academy campus, we lived in former military barracks. Erected in 1938, they weren't built to last. Yet there we were, seventy years after their construction, with our moving van pulling up to a long narrow building that had once housed soldiers during World War II.

What 904A Monterey Drive lacked in style, it more than made up for in scenery. Our living room picture window proudly displayed a panoramic view of the Pacific Ocean. Some afternoons, when the sun sparkled on the waves, the glints of light were so bright, we'd say, "The diamonds are out today!" And the sunsets . . . oh, the sunsets! "We live in a $100 shack with a $100 million view!" we often joked.

The beauty before us made it easy to forget not only the

austerity of our home, but also its original purpose. We were reminded one day when Daniel was trying to drill through the floor of his home office so he could run new Internet wiring.

The barracks sat on stilts, raised a few feet off the ground, and he'd had no trouble drilling through the living room floor or the kids' bedroom floors and running the wires underneath. But he broke bit after bit trying to drill through the floor of his office. Finally, he ripped up the carpet, pulled up a floorboard, and saw the problem: He was trying to drill through a concrete slab.

Talking with the "old timers" on campus, we learned that during the war, our entire building had been the infirmary, and Daniel's office had served as the surgery suite.

During that first year, we were constantly surprised to encounter such remainders from the war, both in our home and when out and about the campus. But as the years passed, we got used to seeing huge bunker doors rising up in the midst of organic strawberry fields. We referred to the once majestic Pacific Amphitheater as simply "Beach Auditorium," never really thinking of the Camp McQuaide officers and enlisted men who once sat in the plush seats, enjoying live performances from famous entertainers. The enormous rusted gun turret base cemented into the bluff was merely part of our walkway as we strolled down to the beach.

"We're just here 'suffering for Jesus'!" we'd joke with anyone who asked what it was like to live on a Christian boarding school campus *by the beach*. It was hard to imagine that the same horizon we viewed through our living room window had once been scrutinized by members of the 250th Coast Artillery Regiment for signs of the enemy. And yet, despite the glory of golden sunsets and the percussion of crashing waves, the fact remained: We lived in a place built for war.

In our everyday lives, we each battle a similar dichotomy: the contrast between the ideal and the real. Ecclesiastes 3:11 expresses the paradoxical tension we live in this way: "He has made everything beautiful in its time. He has also set eternity in the human heart." You and I live with dual citizenship: Even as our bodies remain earthbound, our spirits echo with the heartbeat of heaven. So on the one hand, we sing "How Great Thou Art." On the other, we acknowledge "This World Is Not My Home."

It's so easy to get caught up in trying to bring heaven closer to earth, only to feel defeated when it never quite works. We carefully curate our homes, choosing every decoration precisely. But a lack of peace intrudes on our daily lives just the same. We throw ourselves into a new self-improvement plan, certain that *This is the one!* But sooner or later, the same old sense of disappointment beats us down again. We strategize how to "help" our people live up to the potential we just know they have within them. But in the end, they feel invaded while we feel unappreciated.

It's hard living on a broken planet when your heart is set for heaven. And if there's anyone who truly understands this struggle, it's Jesus. He knows what we're going through because He left the ideal: heaven. He came down to the real: earth. And He lived among us as a dual citizen Himself.

So His words "In this world you will have trouble" are zero percent theory, 100 percent reality. But they're not some pessimistic "truth bomb" meant to make us stop being starry-eyed idealists and start being joyless realists. They're actually protection from pessimism. And then Jesus follows up His statement of what's real with an assurance that reaches beyond our grandest ideal: "Take heart! I have overcome the world."

Amidst the daily reminders that we live in a world still at war, we have the promise of peace in Him. We have Jesus Himself, our eternal source of peace.

The Next, Most Faith-Filled Step

Where are you struggling with the contrast between your ideal versus the real in your life?

_____

_____

_____

_____

_____

_____

_____

_____

Creating Space

Speak

Read the passage aloud three times.

Ponder

Take a moment to let the words silently flow over you.

Now, some questions to ponder:

What does the passage say?

Why is God bringing you this passage now?

Who comes to mind as you read this passage?

What thoughts come to mind as you ponder?

_____

_____

_____

_____

_____

_____

_____

_____

_____

_____

_____

_____

_____

Act

Is there something God wants you to do because of reading this verse today?

_____

_____

_____

_____

Commit

What has God committed to you in this verse? What promises or truths can you make room for in your thinking?

_____

_____

_____

_____

_____

Express

Finally, take a moment to express aloud to God how you think and feel about your time making space for this piece of Scripture.

_____

_____

_____

_____

_____

KATHI

A prudent person foresees danger and takes precautions.
The simpleton goes blindly on and suffers the consequences.

PROVERBS 27:12 NLT

When I was waiting for the sale to close on our mountain retreat, I spent a lot of time thinking about walks in the woods with my beloved, picking wildflowers, hosting outdoor barbeques, and gathering up the wild blackberries that grew in abundance on our property.

What I didn't spend as much time—or, let's be clear, any time—thinking about were the hours, days, and weeks we would spend clearing the property of underbrush, chopping down dead trees, watching weather reports, attending fire safety meetings, working at fire safety fundraisers, and doing everything humanly possible to prevent fires at our house and in our forest.

So, much of what we're doing in the mountains is working hard to make sure that we're not the cause, or the casualty, of a fire. A part-time job in fire prevention? That was not featured on the Zillow listing. But I sleep better at night knowing that our little town is not going to end up on the national news as the cause of a California wildfire.

One of the rallying cries I've heard over and over the past few years when it comes to fire—and unemployment, politics, and pandemics—is this: "I will not live in fear!" And I agree . . . to a point.

No, I definitely don't want to live a life shaped by anxiety. I don't want to be the person who *what ifs* every scenario and is constantly on high alert. But I do want to be that person who understands that fear truly can be a gift.

I'm grateful God has given me ways to sense when danger is coming and to prepare for it. I'm grateful God has also given me unseen ways (both the Holy Spirit and my gut) to sense that there is something off in a situation and to take proper action.

Here's how I see it: When there's a situation, fear can often be the initial response. That's okay. There's some scary stuff happening in the world. But after the initial fear, I have two directions I can go.

First, I can hang on to the fear and not deal with it. Fear that's not addressed turns quickly into anxiety. Some of the telltale signs:

- Feeling nervous, restless, or tense
- A sense of impending danger, panic, or doom

- An increased heart rate
- Trouble concentrating or thinking about anything other than the present worry
- Trouble sleeping
- Difficulty controlling worry

At times in my life, I've lived with overwhelming anxiety. I felt like I had to get on with life, but, at the same time, I was stuck in a place of not really being able to think about other things because of my overwhelming anxiety.

But we have another choice besides anxiety. We can choose the path God has set out for us, and that is wisdom. Philippians 4:6-7 tells us, "Do not be anxious about anything, but in every situation, by prayer and petition, with thanksgiving, present your requests to God. And the peace of God, which transcends all understanding, will guard your hearts and your minds in Christ Jesus."

So we can pray. And we can thank God for our circumstances. And we can be protected from false teaching.

We can listen to experts. We can seek out knowledge. And we can find the truth.

What I especially love is that when I do take precautions—whether it's taking my vitamins, staying home when I'm sick, or getting those batteries changed in the smoke detectors—it lessens my anxiety. There's an old saying: "Trust God and tie up your horse." God expects us to trust Him with our lives. That's where faith comes in. And God trusts us to use the knowledge we have and make good decisions with it. That's where wisdom comes in. Living a life marked by faith and wisdom is a beautiful partnership with God.

Faith doesn't mean I can do whatever I want because God is some kind of magical cleanup crew, following behind me to take care of the consequences. Faith means I follow God on the path of wisdom. I do the things He tells me to do, and I use wisdom in the areas He doesn't spell out in His Word.

I'm grateful for the gift of fear. Fear helps me know what to pay attention to. And I'm grateful for the gift of wisdom. Wisdom helps me take steps of faith instead of being stuck in anxiety.

The Next, Most Faith-Filled Step

There is something causing each of us anxiety in our lives. Hey, we're human. Is there an opportunity, right now, to turn that anxiety into wisdom in action?

Throughout this book, we're asking you to take the next, most faith-filled step. That is what wisdom is: seeking God and asking Him what that next step is. In that area that is bringing you anxiety, what exactly is your next faith-filled step—a choice that may be hard but that you know God is calling you to make?

_____

_____

_____

_____

_____

Now, break it down. What is something you can do in the next
five minutes to move forward? Ask a friend for support? Ask your
husband for time to plan? Do an initial Google search for more
information?

_____

_____

_____

_____

_____

Spend the next five minutes doing that step, because anxiety
lessens when we put wisdom into action.

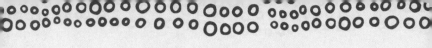

Creating Space

Speak

Read the passage aloud three times.

Ponder

Take a moment to let the words silently flow over you.

Now, some questions to ponder:

What does the passage say?

Why is God bringing you this passage now?

Who comes to mind as you read this passage?

What thoughts come to mind as you ponder?

_____

_____

_____

_____

_____

_____

_____

_____

_____

_____

_____

_____

_____

Act

Is there something God wants you to do because of reading this verse today?

_____

_____

_____

_____

Commit

What has God committed to you in this verse? What promises or truths can you make room for in your thinking?

_____

_____

_____

_____

_____

Express

Finally, take a moment to express aloud to God how you think and feel about your time making space for this piece of Scripture.

_____

_____

_____

_____

_____

CHERI

*He will not let your foot slip—he who watches over you
will not slumber; indeed, he who watches over Israel
will neither slumber nor sleep. The* Lord *watches over
you—the* Lord *is your shade at your right hand; the
sun will not harm you by day, nor the moon by night.*

PSALM 121:3-6

How did it get so hot?

I stared at the stove, trying to make sense of what I was seeing. Somehow, the black plastic handle of my tiny coffeepot had melted away from its aluminum lid and dropped onto the glowing red burner, which now billowed black smoke.

In a dreamlike trance, I turned off the stove, grabbed a wooden spoon, and scooted both the pot and melted handle off the burner before it burst into flame. I threw open the kitchen windows and front door, hoping to prevent the smoke detector from screaming in protest. I reached into the freezer for a handful of ice cubes and put a few on the burner. They melted instantly. I rubbed one over the coffeepot. This cube, too, was reduced to water in seconds.

How did it get so hot?

Slowly, my brain fog cleared, and the answer became clear: I forgot to add water to the pot before putting it on the burner and turning it up to high.

As I noticed that the paint on my new coffeepot has changed from bright red to dark brown, the full implications of what I'd done—and what could have happened—dawned on me. *If I'd walked out of the kitchen for even a minute . . .*

I closed my eyes and shook my head at the thought.

An hour later, after airing out the house, I debated whether to tell my husband and adult children, "Hey, guess how close I came to burning down the house today?" What I'd done was embarrassing, and we're a family of kidders. My son regularly refers to the smoke alarm as "Mom's kitchen timer."

When I did share the incident with my husband and adult children, I confessed, "I must be more exhausted than I realized. I don't remember not adding the water. I just sort of sleepwalked through the whole process until I saw the handle melting off the coffeepot."

This was one of many wake-up calls during a very hard season. I felt like a zombie much of the time. I wasn't as aware of the people in my life as I used to be. I became withdrawn. It took all my energy not to shut down completely.

It's such a relief to know that this doesn't happen to God. He doesn't become exhausted. He never sleepwalks, never goes numb, never shuts down. God never gets overwhelmed. Like the waves of the Pacific Ocean that never stop tumbling to shore, God is constant. He "will never slumber nor sleep." He is always attentive, ever on high alert. He's on duty so we can rest.

When I was a child and woke up afraid in the middle of the night, my dad would hear me crying into my pillow and come check on me. He'd pull up a chair next to my bed and listen as I described the bad dream I'd just had or the scary noise I'd heard outside my window. He never belittled my fears. Instead, he'd tell me, "You go to sleep. I'll stay right here." He'd leave on a small light and sit with me. I'd close my eyes for a little while. And then I'd peek with one eye. *He's still here.* A few minutes later, I'd peek again. *He's still here.* At some point, I'd quit peeking and fall back asleep.

It's such a comfort to know that the same Almighty Creator who hung the moon in the sky is also my Abba Father who watches over me with the never-ending constancy of ocean tides. Because of His attentiveness, He knows every little detail of who I am and what I'm experiencing.

And He also knows that my hesitation to tell my family about the coffeepot incident wasn't over a little good-natured ribbing. He knows my reluctance was because I forgot something so incredibly obvious. He knows that for someone who watched her mother say the "long goodbye" of Alzheimer's disease, such a memory lapse isn't just embarrassing; it's absolutely terrifying.

He knows, and He's still here.

"The Lord watches over you—the Lord is your shade at your right hand; the sun will not harm you by day, nor the moon by night." He is our eternal light in darkness. He knows our vulnerabilities, our fears, and even our terrors. And He stands guard.

The thing that just happened that you're fretting about? He knows, and He's still here.

This hard season you're in? He knows, and He's still here.

That secret fear? He knows, and He's still here.

He's on duty. Cry out to Him. Tell Him all about it. So you *can* rest.

The Next, Most Faith-Filled Step

The thing that just happened that you're fretting about? This hard season you're in? That secret fear? Take a moment to process what's happening in your head and in your heart right here.

_____

_____

_____

_____

_____

_____

_____

Creating Space

Speak

Read the passage aloud three times.

Ponder

Take a moment to let the words silently flow over you.

Now, some questions to ponder:

    What does the passage say?

    Why is God bringing you this passage now?

    Who comes to mind as you read this passage?

    What thoughts come to mind as you ponder?

_____

_____

_____

_____

_____

_____

_____

_____

_____

_____

_____

_____

_____

Act

Is there something God wants you to do because of reading this verse today?

_____

_____

_____

_____

Commit

What has God committed to you in this verse? What promises or truths can you make room for in your thinking?

_____

_____

_____

_____

_____

Express

Finally, take a moment to express aloud to God how you think and feel about your time making space for this piece of Scripture.

_____

_____

_____

_____

_____

KATHI

Commit to the LORD whatever you do,
and he will establish your plans.

PROVERBS 16:3

I am a sucker for a good makeover show.

I don't care what you're making over: a room, a house, a business, a person . . . Give me 60 minutes on basic cable with a couple of bossy experts and an unlimited budget, and I'm in. I love the idea that with a few tweaks, some expert advice, and a little bit of creativity, anything and anyone is redeemable.

When we finally owned the Red House, I had a long list of projects I wanted to get done to not only make the house our own but also to make it suitable for us to host writer retreats for large groups. Plus, the previous owners used this as a second home. We were going to need to make some changes since we planned on living here year-round.

Yes! We were going to come up with our own makeover show, minus the experts, the budget, and the cameras. Roger and I came up with my long list of all the DIY projects I wanted to get accomplished, and we set to work.

And here is what I discovered about weekend DIY projects—they never, ever, take just a weekend. Here's what I've learned about these "quick and easy" household projects:

1. *Plans are always more involved than they first seem.* When you watch someone on a YouTube video build a chicken coop, it takes them about 30 minutes. Even with that, we knew it would be easier to buy a kit, so that's what we did.

Turns out the kit was way more involved than just building it ourselves. The instructions said an amateur woodworker would take four hours to complete it. Roger is well beyond amateur, and it took sixteen hours. In other words, the company *lied.*

But no matter. Roger went in with a great attitude and built a run to go with the chicken coop, and now our girls have a home that would be the envy of any feathered fowl in the mountains. But let's be clear—it's never as simple as they say it's going to be.

2. *Your conditions are different from the ones the Pinterest girl lives in.* So Pinterest Patti is creating a business around the painted flower boxes she makes, and she assures you that you can as well. What Patti failed to mention is that her husband is a woodworking expert and has every drill and router known to man (and you thought a router was just something you used to get Internet so you could watch her videos . . .).

3. *Your skill level is different.* You as a first-time gardener are going to make a lot more mistakes than someone whose professional name is Sunflower.

But I think the most important thing I've discovered when it comes to projects is this: My forethought needs some work.

A good DIY project brings out a difference in Roger and me: Roger is a planner, while I'm a more of a "let's get started and see how it goes" kinda girl. I have discovered that what I used to be able to get away with when I lived in town is much harder to get away with here in the mountains. When Home Depot was six minutes from my house, I could go there half a dozen times for a project, and it wasn't a huge deal. Now, a round trip to Home Depot takes four hours and wastes most of a day.

As it goes with DIY projects, so it goes with the rest of my life. While I will never be a natural planner, I have realized that when I go to God first with my plans (instead of barreling through and asking God to clean up my mess) it works better for everyone involved. (Most surprised by this concept? Me.)

When we commit our plans to the Lord, what we are actually committing to is trusting God with our next steps. God knows what we need to move forward, and He knows the obstacles we are going to come up against. I also believe that having the right plan means knowing when the Holy Spirit is asking you to change something up, stop something, or start something different on your plan.

When I began to study and read commentary on Proverbs 16:3—"Commit to the LORD whatever you do, and he will establish your plans"—what I loved most about it is that when we commit our plans to God, we're not just asking Him to rubber stamp our plans with a "YAY" or a veto. Our goal is to have our plans be God's plans that He has already established for us. This is us cosigning onto God's plan, not God cosigning onto ours.

There is something so freeing about praying over and committing our plans to God before we get started on anything. Asking God to reveal the flaws in our plans before we start. Asking God to care for us amid setbacks, failure, and frustrations. Asking God to guide us through our own limited human thinking and help us see our path in supernatural ways. All these prayers ensure we don't sit in the failures alone, and that when it comes time to celebrate the victories, we give the glory to the One who saw us through.

The Next, Most Faith-Filled Step

I am famous for barreling ahead and consulting God in the rearview mirror. So today, join me in stopping, waiting, and listening.

Is there something you are planning to do in your life? Is there a change you are planning to make in your family, career, or relationships?

_____

_____

_____

Stop with me and present it to God. And then wait. Over the next few days, keep bringing that plan to God. And then wait some more.

Creating Space

Speak
Read the passage aloud three times.

Ponder
Take a moment to let the words silently flow over you.

Now, some questions to ponder:

What does the passage say?

Why is God bringing you this passage now?

Who comes to mind as you read this passage?

What thoughts come to mind as you ponder?

_____

_____

_____

_____

_____

_____

_____

_____

_____

_____

_____

_____

Act

Is there something God wants you to do because of reading this verse today?

_____

_____

_____

_____

Commit

What has God committed to you in this verse? What promises or truths can you make room for in your thinking?

_____

_____

_____

_____

_____

Express

Finally, take a moment to express aloud to God how you think and feel about your time making space for this piece of Scripture.

_____

_____

_____

_____

_____

Strengthening through Stretching

CHERI

*We also glory in our sufferings, because we know
that suffering produces perseverance; perseverance,
character; and character, hope. And hope does not
put us to shame, because God's love has been
poured out into our hearts through the
Holy Spirit, who has been given to us.*

ROMANS 5:3-5

Twenty years ago I walked into the gym, ready for a good
workout. An hour later, I walked out feeling as though
someone had stabbed me in the back with a hot knife. I endured
months of persistent pain before learning I'd fractured my T7
vertebra and herniated the discs above and below it.

During those months, I was so scared of the pain I was feeling
and so terrified of making it worse that I shrank into self-protection
mode. I felt fragile, breakable, like one wrong would shatter me. So
I froze, becoming tense, rigid, resistant to movement. At first, this
was an intentional choice; soon, it became an unconscious habit.

Eventually, I saw a sports specialist and discovered the cause of my continuing pain. Muscle knots had formed all around the site of my original injury. This meant the pain I was feeling was no longer from the fracture. Instead, I was feeling the sharp spasms of muscles that were on a valiant but misguided mission to hold me together. My determination to stay still, lying on the couch and moving as little as possible, was all wrong.

Instead of self-protection, I needed to strengthen.

So my doctor sent me to physical therapy, where I was the worst possible patient during my first session. All I could think was *After all this pain and all this time off work, she'd better fix me fast!* But the only thing that happened quickly that day was my plummet from hope to despair when my PT told me how many months she expected my healing to take.

During our initial appointments, I could hardly move. But as I practiced a series of small, slow, steady stretches, my physical therapist assigned harder ones. Day by day, my range of motion increased and my pain level decreased.

Two decades after my back injury, I still use the exact same stretches to keep chronic pain at bay. When I don't do them, the pain builds, I start to feel fragile, and I face the same choice all over again: *Will I stay rigid and unmoving? Or will I trust that stretching leads to strengthening?*

My natural reaction to any form of pain is to freeze for fear that I'll break. But I'm learning—in all areas of life—that God did not make us fragile. He created us flexible.

The sequence we find in Romans 5:3-5 reminds me of the stretching I went through during physical therapy: "Suffering produces perseverance; perseverance, character; and character, hope." Honestly, this does not sound like fun. Yet I absolutely recognize the truth of this progression.

Is there an area of your life that feels frozen right now? A situation in which you feel so fragile, you've become rigid and unmoving? Where instead of self-protection, you need to strengthen? God did not make you fragile. He created you flexible, able to stretch and strengthen physically, spiritually, and relationally.

Physically. Notice what parts of your body need to be stretched more often. When you exercise, are you intentional about stretching before and after? When you're doing deskwork, do you take regular stretch breaks? Could you use a new stretching tool, such as a foam roll or elastic bands? Dismiss any all-or-nothing thinking as it arises and remember: small, slow, and steady. As you see incremental progress, celebrate each small victory along the way.

Spiritually. Invite God to show you one area of your spiritual life that feels stuck. You may feel the pain in one area, but like a good physical therapist, He's skilled at detecting where the real problem lies. Whatever the specific area of spiritual atrophy, trust Him to guide you in small, slow, and steady ways. As you continually feel stretched just beyond your comfort zone, remember: This is the goal! And it's evidence of God's transforming power at work within you.

Relationally. Identify one place in your relationships where you're especially rigid. Pray for the courage to lean into the pain of breaking up old destructive habits and developing new healthy ones. As other people resist the changes you're making, remember: You don't need self-protection; you need to strengthen. Also, avoid any urge to attempt an overnight overhaul of your entire life. Focus on that one rigid place, keeping your stretches small, slow, and steady.

Careful stretching will not cause you to shatter. It will show you what you're already capable of but didn't yet know. When you start small, slow, and steady, stretching won't break you. It will help you to continue to strengthen, heal, and grow.

The Next, Most Faith-Filled Step

Think of an area of your life that feels frozen right now—a situation in which you've felt so fragile, you've become rigid and unmoving. How can you start stretching in ways that are . . .

small: _____

_____

slow: _____

_____

steady: _____

_____

Creating Space

Speak

Read the passage aloud three times.

Ponder

Take a moment to let the words silently flow over you.

Now, some questions to ponder:

What does the passage say?

Why is God bringing you this passage now?

Who comes to mind as you read this passage?

What thoughts come to mind as you ponder?

_____

_____

_____

_____

_____

_____

_____

_____

_____

_____

_____

_____

_____

Act

Is there something God wants you to do because of reading this
verse today?

_____

_____

_____

_____

Commit

What has God committed to you in this verse? What promises or
truths can you make room for in your thinking?

_____

_____

_____

_____

Express

Finally, take a moment to express aloud to God how you think
and feel about your time making space for this piece of Scripture.

_____

_____

_____

_____

_____

Working It Out

KATHI

May the favor of the Lord our God rest on us;
establish the work of our hands for us—
yes, establish the work of our hands.

PSALM 90:17

While visiting our cabin in the mountains can be a magical experience, what it takes to keep it running may not be obvious at first glance—or, let's be honest, until after signing the mortgage paperwork and living there through the first winter. Besides our regular jobs, there's always a long list of things that absolutely must be done: clearing brush, taking down dead trees, chopping firewood, cooking meals, changing sheets, cleaning the chicken coop. And it feels like we are forever preparing for the next season.

When we started to have guests at the Red House, we learned to invite people with a caveat: In the morning, we will cook you a glorious breakfast (for which the chickens have provided the main ingredient) and keep the coffeepot full. In the evenings, we will have cheese and crackers around the fire and then settle in for a wonderful dinner and talking late into the night (with more coffee).

However, from after breakfast until cracker time, Roger and I are either working at our jobs or working on the mountain. We used to try to "get ahead" on work and mountain chores before guests arrived, but it seems that "getting ahead" lasts for less than a day, and there we are again, behind on all the things that need to be done. It turns out there is no such thing as "caught up" or "getting ahead" around here. So there is never a day to take off and just hang out with people. And we are simply fine with the tradeoff of living in paradise and getting to be its caretaker.

But not everyone understands our deal with Mother Nature, so we explain it in advance: Please entertain yourself from the hours of eight a.m. to five p.m. And our guests happily agree; they like visiting paradise as well.

As we have given these instructions, we've learned there are three kinds of guests who come to the Red House to get away from it all.

The first are those who come to relax. They want to sit by the fire, eat good food, and walk in the woods—or just read a book about walking in the woods. And we love that kind of guest. We love to spoil those who are wearied by the world and just need a place of respite. And don't we all need that at some point in our lives? Maybe work has been extra challenging, or caring for kids or aging parents has taken its toll. Sometimes, we just need to rest and be restored.

But we have been surprised to find that the most common visitor we have at the Red House is the one who wants to get in on the action. They want to know how to clean the chicken coop, chop logs on the mountain and bring them back to the woodshed, cook dinner for the crew, or do one of the other 947 things that need to be done at any time. At first, I was completely surprised. I thought everyone we invited would want to get away to the mountains to relax. But it is surprising how many people want to come and swing an ax.

Then there is a third kind of guest. The one who comes declaring, "I don't want to do anything but sit by the fire, read a book, and pet the dog." And we assure them that their plan is a fine plan. But after a day or two of deep fire sitting, a strange thing starts to happen. Our proclaimed fire-sitter starts to look for things to work on. Maybe it's planting some vegetables for spring, baking some muffins, or just sweeping the floor of the kitchen. After some rest, people often want to work.

Popular culture has taught us that the goal is not to work. To be free from responsibility and burden. To be able to do what we want, when we want. That relaxation is the ultimate reward. But most people, I have come to find out, actually love to work. (And here I thought I was the weirdo.)

God has designed us for work. When we are in a healthy place, work not only isn't a burden; it can be downright soul satisfying. To know you've improved life for those you love—even if they're chickens—is good for the soul. To have accomplished something, to have served someone else, or to make something a little better than we found it? God has ordained it, and our soul longs for it.

We have had guests come up and beg to freshen the chicken run and haul logs. We have had friends "come to relax" by helping build a greenhouse. On a notable day, Roger mentioned that he wanted some steps to go up out of the mountain to another landing. Our friend Scott grabbed a shovel and started to carve out stairs into the mountain.

What inside a person makes them want to take time off from their job, only to come to the mountain to break a sweat? You, my friend, are a reflection of God, the Creator. God designed us for work and creation. God designed work to be good for us, good for our soul. God knew we needed direction and purpose. He "established the work of our hands" so our souls could be satisfied.

The Next, Most Faith-Filled Step

How do you feel about work? Does the thought of it weigh you down or bring satisfaction to your soul?

_____

_____

_____

_____

_____

_____

_____

_____

_____

_____

_____

If just the thought of work exhausts you, it may be time to find a path to some deep rest. Trading childcare for a day a week to spend part of that day resting. A three-day weekend without plans, just rest. A talk with your doctor about your sleep patterns or more. Rest is not a luxury, and work shouldn't always be a burden.

Creating Space

Speak

Read the passage aloud three times.

Ponder

Take a moment to let the words silently flow over you.

Now, some questions to ponder:

> What does the passage say?
>
> Why is God bringing you this passage now?
>
> Who comes to mind as you read this passage?
>
> What thoughts come to mind as you ponder?

_____

_____

_____

_____

_____

_____

_____

_____

_____

_____

_____

_____

_____

_____

Act

Is there something God wants you to do because of reading this verse today?

_____

_____

_____

_____

Commit

What has God committed to you in this verse? What promises or truths can you make room for in your thinking?

_____

_____

_____

_____

_____

Express

Finally, take a moment to express aloud to God how you think and feel about your time making space for this piece of Scripture.

_____

_____

_____

_____

_____

Kikuyu Grass

CHERI

You have hedged me behind and before,
and laid Your hand upon me.
Such knowledge is too wonderful for me;
it is high, I cannot attain it.

PSALM 139:5-6 NKJV

There's grass growing *inside* our wall!"

We had just started a long-overdue home improvement project: replacing a rotten windowsill. As we pried the crumbling boards away, the inside of the wall was exposed and unexpected greenery sprang into view.

Peering into the wall space, I wondered, *What kind of grass grows where there's no light?*

The answer, I soon learned, is kikuyu grass. Kikuyu is a fast-growing grass that's not native to California—it came from Africa. When damaged, it repairs itself quickly, making it an ideal ground cover for a military base or a boarding school. Incredibly durable, it easily resists the wear and tear of people walking on it, sports teams playing games on it, even cars driving and parking on it.

It's also a federal noxious weed:

> Kikuyu is sold in some states with restrictions
> that have to be followed to prevent the grass
> from spreading beyond its desired location.
> Kikuyu grass is not a good option near gardens
> because it is so invasive. It spreads quickly un-
> der the ground and can easily invade areas
> outside of the lawn.*

I've started noticing kikuyu grass all sorts of places it doesn't belong in our neighborhood: poking out of mailboxes, snaking through gutters, crawling down into chimneys.

Kikuyu grass is like the holiday celebration that morphs into an unmanageable calendar of activities. The simple home repair project that blows up into a full-scale remodel. The quick stop at the mall that becomes a credit card spending spree. The cascade of over-eager "yeses" to requests, invitations, and "new opportunities."

Of course, there's nothing inherently wrong with holidays, home repair, shopping, or helping others. When these experiences flourish within healthy bounds, they can be truly wonderful—for you and those you love. Problems arise when they become invasive.

"Kikuyu Grass Facts, Maintenance & Comparison," ProGardenTips, March 23, 2021, www.progardentips.com/kikuyu-grass.

Some signs that you're suddenly dealing with a noxious weed in your life:

- feeling depleted
- a rising sense of panic
- unnecessary debt
- increasing clutter
- a packed schedule with little-to-no margin left
- bitterness and resentment

If you want to stop the spread of invasive overwhelm, you've got to define the edges of your lawn—which is easier said than done. But the same God who planted a hedge of protection around David offers us a hedge of protection through His Word. James 1:5 promises, "If any of you lacks wisdom, you should ask God, who gives generously to all without finding fault, and it will be given to you."

Truth be told, I don't always like the wisdom God offers. Sometimes I become downright grouchy when He makes it clear to me that something I really, *really* want is, in fact, a noxious weed. In such moments, a deep urge to *Do it anyway!* wells up within me. As if somehow I know better than God. Not in general, of course, but in this particular situation . . . And I have to recognize, for the umpteenth time, that at the root of all the "kikuyu grass" that invades my life is my own greedy craving to #DoAllTheThings.

I have spent too much of my life trying to cheat the system: attempting to live without limits or consequences. If you have too, then you know how high a price we pay for living this way. So I pray constantly for God's hedge of protection by seeking His wisdom. To remind my prone-to-wander heart to stay within the bounds of where God has "hedged me behind and before." To remind my ever-busy body to stay where His hand is upon me rather than dashing off to chase another new shiny object or opportunity.

And I keep a simple journal. In it, I write out my prayers asking God to help me discern between His invitation and an invasion. I chronicle His responses and my own reactions. And I track the results of staying within His hedge of protection, of choosing to remain with His hand upon me.

Keeping record of how often my own reactions are flat-out wrong is humbling. It helps me think twice before deciding that "Do it anyway!" or "In this particular situation . . ." are worthy ideas because I have so much hard evidence they aren't. It helps kill all forms of "kikuyu grass" at the root.

More importantly, documenting the good that happens when I stay within God's hedge of protection increases my trust in His benevolent omniscience. Even as I agree with the psalmist, "Such knowledge is too wonderful for me; it is high, I cannot attain it," my faith in God's promised protection is strengthened by what I do see.

The Next, Most Faith-Filled Step

Ask these two simple questions about the area of your life that feels most overwhelming right now:

What is my kikuyu grass?

Where has it invaded?

_____

_____

_____

_____

_____

_____

_____

_____

_____

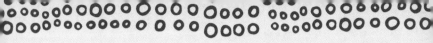

Creating Space

Speak

Read the passage aloud three times.

Ponder

Take a moment to let the words silently flow over you.

Now, some questions to ponder:

What does the passage say?

Why is God bringing you this passage now?

Who comes to mind as you read this passage?

What thoughts come to mind as you ponder?

_____

_____

_____

_____

_____

_____

_____

_____

_____

_____

_____

_____

_____

Act

Is there something God wants you to do because of reading this verse today?

_____

_____

_____

_____

Commit

What has God committed to you in this verse? What promises or truths can you make room for in your thinking?

_____

_____

_____

_____

_____

Express

Finally, take a moment to express aloud to God how you think and feel about your time making space for this piece of Scripture.

_____

_____

_____

_____

_____

Pain in the Neck

KATHI

*In their hearts humans plan their course,
but the LORD establishes their steps.*

PROVERBS 16:9

It started as a little pain in my shoulder. You know—the kind that's just a little hitch. It catches you unaware every once in a while.

Then, it seized hold of my neck—to the point that I couldn't sleep, it was just that uncomfortable.

And then, the next day, when I was driving our Jeep with the large trailer, I realized I couldn't turn my head to look what was coming from the left. (And when you're driving a Jeep with a large trailer? It's really helpful to know what's coming from the left.) I woke up the next morning after a terrible night's sleep, unable to move my head from the left to the right even a little bit.

You never know how important your neck is until you cannot use it.

I don't even remember doing anything to strain my neck. It was just one of those things that comes out of the blue and wreaks havoc on not only your body, but your schedule. So at first I did all the holistic stuff you are supposed to do — ice and then warm compresses, rest, lots of water. And then I gave up and took the drugs that make you sleep like a teenage boy on the first day of summer vacation.

And I slept.

And I slept.

And I slept.

But the pain persisted.

I kept searching the Internet for the magical neck stretch I could do to make everything feel better. Was there a food that helped in muscle recovery? Or maybe a patch I could put on my neck to magically make me feel better?

You see, this wasn't a very good time for me to rest. I had a deadline; I had people relying on me. And I needed to get better. Now. Like everyone else on the planet over the age of 30, I have had some traumatic experiences in my life. And my personality says, *Let's just heal from this and move on as fast as we possibly can, shall we? I don't have time for this trauma — I have a lot to get accomplished.*

I bet you've felt the same. You want to recover faster. People want you to recover faster. I have in my mind exactly how long the healing should take: "Give me a good night's sleep and I'll be ready to roll tomorrow!" But here is the problem I keep coming up against: We don't get to determine how long healing should take. I am not someone who likes to dwell, but here is what I know about healing—none of us gets to skip steps.

With my neck, I have to do all that stupid stuff doctors say you have to do to heal. And maybe when it comes to emotional healing, you really want to skip that "stupid stuff" like steps that require you dredge up the past. Or maybe confronting the person who hurt you is the step you'd like to skip.

Even when I don't like where the steps are taking me, and when I don't like how slow a pace they're taking, God's the One who determines them. And that is why it is so critical to have people around you who can see your frustration, but will keep showing you that God is doing what God does, and that you are healing, and you are making progress.

Keep people around you who don't rush your healing. Who allow you to take the time you need, even if it's inconvenient for them. When my neck first started to give me problems, Roger reminded me he had had a similar experience. And then he proceeded to remind me not only was he barely functioning for two weeks, but he had to go to the emergency room to get pain meds. So every time I felt so much guilt about not being able to take care of our chickens, or making that night's dinner, Roger would remind me, "Two weeks and a trip to the ER." What he was actually saying was, "You've been hurt. I've been there. I know it takes time to heal. I will be here to do the heavy lifting until you go through the process of healing."

You want people around you who are not going to rush your

recovery. Who are going to sit with you, in your pain, and ask you if you need another warm compress or a cup of coffee. And most of the time, that is someone who has been though the trauma and has healed from it. They remember what healing looks like, how long it takes, and that sometimes, time is the most important component.

One of the most important lessons I've learned through all of this is not to rush someone else's healing. But I will admit, there have been times I've wanted to rush someone's recovery because it was hard for me to watch. I don't like to see people in pain. I don't like to see people I love sit in their suffering. But often, that is exactly where they need to be. And I need to be brave enough to sit with them.

The Next, Most Faith-Filled Step

Is there a step you are trying to skip in healing that is keeping you stuck? Spend a moment getting uncomfortable with knowing what you need to do but don't want to do in your healing.

_____

_____

_____

_____

_____

_____

_____

Then, ask God to help you take that next, most faith-filled step. Maybe it's not calling the person to apologize—yet. Maybe it's writing down what you want to say, or practicing with a friend. You don't have to take all the scary steps at once. Just the next small one.

Creating Space

Speak

Read the passage aloud three times.

Ponder

Take a moment to let the words silently flow over you.

Now, some questions to ponder:

What does the passage say?

Why is God bringing you this passage now?

Who comes to mind as you read this passage?

What thoughts come to mind as you ponder?

_____

_____

_____

_____

_____

_____

_____

_____

_____

_____

_____

_____

Act

Is there something God wants you to do because of reading this verse today?

_____

_____

_____

_____

Commit

What has God committed to you in this verse? What promises or truths can you make room for in your thinking?

_____

_____

_____

_____

_____

Express

Finally, take a moment to express aloud to God how you think and feel about your time making space for this piece of Scripture.

_____

_____

_____

_____

_____

Purr-fect Trust

CHERI

The LORD is my strength and my shield;
my heart trusts in him, and he helps me.
My heart leaps for joy, and with
my song I praise him.

PSALM 28:7

I was not a cat person. Then my daughter brought home an orange tabby kitten named Rafiki. The runt of his litter, he made up for his itty-bitty size with an enormous purr that rendered me powerless to resist him.

I'd walk into a room, unaware he was there, only to be greeted by a crescendo of celebratory vibrations. I'd sit down to pet him for just a moment. And hours later, I'd still be there, covered in cat fur, unable to move, a tiny orange "purr box" happily ensconced on my lap.

A few years ago, I noticed that something wasn't quite right with Rafiki. He looked thin, and he was always drinking. When I took him in to the vet, I was stunned by the diagnosis—feline diabetes—and overwhelmed by the treatment plan: insulin shots twice a day, plus around-the-clock blood testing to monitor his glucose levels.

I drove home from the vet in tears, partly of regret that I'd not caught Rafiki's condition sooner, but mostly of anxiety. I'd always been so squeamish about needles. I'd made my husband take our kids to the dentist when they were little. Now, out of the blue, I needed to give shots and draw blood multiple times a day . . . or my little buddy would die.

A vet tech had shown me how to administer the insulin shots, and I felt confident that with enough practice on an orange, I could master this new skill. But how would I manage the many ear pricks required for blood testing?

As I opened up the new glucose meter and read the directions, my fear mushroomed. I was afraid of hurting Rafiki with my amateur attempts at drawing his blood. I was scared that he'd freak out and scratch me to shreds. Most of all, I was worried he'd become terrified of me—that every treatment would be a fight after which he'd run away and hide from me. Considering how many times per day I'd be coming at him with something sharp, I wouldn't blame him if he ended up hating me.

But after a few false starts, we quickly settled into a routine. As I laid the equipment on the table, Rafiki would hop right up. And instead of squirming, he'd start purring. Soon, he'd begin to purr whenever he heard me simply open his diabetes supply drawer.

"I wonder if he knows," I asked my husband, who has been a cat person since birth. "I wonder if he realizes that all this jabbing and stabbing is what's helping him feel better."

"Maybe," Daniel replied. "I just think he totally trusts you."

I long to trust God the way Rafiki trusts me. Because I've done to God the very thing I feared from Rafiki: I've scratched, fought, run, and hid. Demanding that He answer my questions to my satisfaction before I'll trust Him, I have exhausted myself and distanced from Him.

But God can no more explain to me the intricacies of what is or isn't happening in my life any more than I can explain to Rafiki how insulin works or why he can't have a self-feeder anymore. To trust God to be "my strength and my shield," I need to remember that He is omnipotent and omniscient . . . and I am not.

Each time Rafiki demonstrates his trust in me by hopping up on the table and cooperating with me, I am able to help him. Likewise, when I cooperate with God, I am better able to receive His help. God respects my freedom too much to force His help on me. When "my heart trusts in him"—not in other people, not in myself, but in God alone—"he helps me."

I don't know if cats experience actual joy, but it sure sounds to me as if Rafiki does! I love it when I simply walk into the room or reach for his glucose meter, and he starts purring loudly enough to trigger the San Andreas Fault. He inspires me.

Commenting on Psalm 28:7, author and pastor Henry Spence Jones explains that David is reaching into his "store of song" to offer "thanksgiving for a mercy not yet received." Like David—and like Rafiki!—I want to trust God so fully that "my heart leaps for joy" at the very hint of His presence, and I begin to praise Him for what He's doing. Even when I'm not yet sure exactly what it is.*

Note: Happily, after several months of treatment and dietary changes, Rafiki's diabetes went into remission. I still test his glucose a couple of times a week, and he still leaps onto the table while purring loudly enough to shake the windows and walls!

The Next, Most Faith-Filled Step

When it comes to trusting God, in what ways have you scratched, fought, run, or hid?

_____

_____

_____

_____

How could you demonstrate your trust in God with a heart that leaps for joy and a song of praise today?

_____

_____

_____

_____

---

* H.D.M. Spence Jones, *The Complete Pulpit Commentary, Volume 8: The Psalms* (Grand Rapids, MI: Eerdmans Publishing Company, 1950), Psalm 28:7.

Creating Space

Speak
Read the passage aloud three times.

Ponder
Take a moment to let the words silently flow over you.

Now, some questions to ponder:

What does the passage say?

Why is God bringing you this passage now?

Who comes to mind as you read this passage?

What thoughts come to mind as you ponder?

_____

_____

_____

_____

_____

_____

_____

_____

_____

_____

_____

_____

_____

Act

Is there something God wants you to do because of reading this verse today?

_____

_____

_____

_____

Commit

What has God committed to you in this verse? What promises or truths can you make room for in your thinking?

_____

_____

_____

_____

_____

Express

Finally, take a moment to express aloud to God how you think and feel about your time making space for this piece of Scripture.

_____

_____

_____

_____

_____

A Life Built on Gratitude

KATHI

Give thanks in all circumstances;
for this is God's will for you in Christ Jesus.

1 THESSALONIANS 5:18

One of the first things I do every day is go out to the coop to say a cheery "Good morning!" to the ladies in the Fluffy Butt Hut. I open the run door so they can be the early birds who catch the first-choice worms of the morning, and then I collect the egg.

First thing in the morning, the one egg that will be there is from Brie. She's our Isa Brown Chicken and the early layer in the group. I put her egg in the large pocket of my oversized sweatshirt and then go over and say, "Brie, thank you for the egg! This is going to be delicious!"

Throughout the morning, while the other girls are running around the outside of our house looking for bugs, Truffles and Cheddar will each take a turn in their nesting box. (Or somewhere in the general proximity. I've found eggs balanced on the two-inch-wide roosting bars in the coop.) And I will thank each of these ladies for what they have contributed.

And you may be thinking, *Good for you, Crazy Chicken Lady.* I feel that. Deeply. If you had told me a year ago that I would be thanking our pets for anything coming out of their backside, I would have said that you did not know me, or my willingness to keep livestock, at all.

But after several years of working too many hours, buying too much convenience, and expecting too much out of life, I was developing a spirit of entitlement. And if there's anything I hate to see in other people, it's entitlement. On me? It felt like a wool suit with shoulder pads—ugly and uncomfortable. I found myself, daily, disappointed in life and in other people. When things did not go perfectly, I held grudges and carried my entitlement on my shoulders for the world to see and admire.

Being impatient with my kids, my husband, and the occasional not-so-nice words to my fellow drivers in town was starting to become my default, not my "bad day." (I am rarely rude to people I don't know, but boy, did my husband get an earful when I got home from the dry cleaner, grocery store, or the PTA meeting.) I was impatient with others while having a long list of excuses ready to whip out and present with a second's notice if anyone dared ask me why I wasn't doing what I knew I needed to do: drop the "too much" in my life.

I've tried a number of different ways to tamp down the sense of entitlement in my own life. I've read about it, prayed about it, felt tremendous guilt about it. And while all of these methods have helped to a certain extent (yes, even feeling guilty about it had an impact), I've realized that the daily practice of radical, seems-a-little-weird-but-okay gratitude was my fastest way to change not just my actions but also the very soul of who I was.

For many of us, the past few years have been hard. Life changingly hard. And, at least for me, it was easy to focus on the oh so many things that were going wrong. But what I understand is this: I may not be able to change my circumstances, but I'm always able to change my response to my circumstances. And the most powerful tool I have to change my attitude? Radical, crazy-looking gratitude.

Thanking the cashier at the grocery store. Thanking my kid for taking the dog for a walk. Thanking my husband on the regular for his part in working so hard to provide for us. Thanking the customer service rep on the phone. Thanking my pastor for the sermon on a Sunday morning. Thanking my neighbor for bringing in a package while I was away. Thanking my daughter for a spontaneous hug. And even thanking the chickens for their contribution to the family meal.

But beyond thanking those around us, we have an opportunity to be intentional about thanking God several times a day as well. We can thank Him for a good night's sleep. The taste of a Honeycrisp apple (they really are the best). His presence in our lives, the food He provides, the places we live, the people we love. What does radical gratitude do for us as followers of Christ? It changes our initial reaction to circumstances, and it changes our perspective.

When a tough situation comes up, we can experience our emotions, we can have our reactions, but then, we must find our way back to a place of gratitude. The less gratitude we practice, the harder it is to find our way to peace. But when we practice gratitude daily, we discover the path back to both joy and peace. It becomes such a well-worn path that we know every bump in the road, every crook in the trail, and we can navigate it assuredly because we are so familiar with it.

The Next, Most Faith-Filled Step

Here's a crazy challenge: Count how many times you say thank you in a day. I've done this on a counter on my phone. (And I'm sure I missed a few, because sometimes it comes out without my thinking about it.)

What counts? Thanking the customer service rep on the phone. Thanking your dog for doing its business on command. Thanking God for the provision of the day. Thanking your kid for doing a chore they are supposed to do anyway. And yes, thanking your chickens for their eggs.

See if you can, at least once a week, break your record for thank yous. I promise you, the more gratitude you pour out, the more you retain.

Creating Space

Speak

Read the passage aloud three times.

Ponder

Take a moment to let the words silently flow over you.

Now, some questions to ponder:

What does the passage say?

Why is God bringing you this passage now?

Who comes to mind as you read this passage?

What thoughts come to mind as you ponder?

_____

_____

_____

_____

_____

_____

_____

_____

_____

_____

_____

_____

Act

Is there something God wants you to do because of reading this verse today?

_____

_____

_____

_____

Commit

What has God committed to you in this verse? What promises or truths can you make room for in your thinking?

_____

_____

_____

_____

_____

Express

Finally, take a moment to express aloud to God how you think and feel about your time making space for this piece of Scripture.

_____

_____

_____

_____

_____

CHERI

Blessed is the one . . . whose delight is in the
law of the LORD. . . . That person is like a tree
planted by streams of water, which yields its
fruit in season and whose leaf does not
wither—whatever they do prospers.

PSALM 1:1-3

The first time a flat of fresh strawberries showed up on our front porch, I didn't know what to make of it. Well, I knew what to *make*—strawberry shortcake with whipped cream, of course! But who had left us such a bounty of berries? There was no note. It was a mystery.

A few weeks later, I came home to find that the "Strawberry Fairy" had visited us once again. This time, we made jam. And I made it my goal to discover the identity of our benefactor. Turns out, the farmer who leased the field near our house had a generous habit of sharing the fruits of his harvest with families in the neighborhood.

Over the next decade, we alternated between berry feasts and famines. We dreamed of strawberries every October through February. And each time our farmer friend brought us the first flat of the year, we celebrated the start of a new strawberry season.

So often, on dreary winter days, I've longed for the fresh, sweet burst of juice in that first bite of a strawberry. But those berry plants can't produce constantly. After giving up their harvest, they rest. Retreat. Build up their stores of sugars so come next spring, when the warm sunlight tells them it's time, they can grow again.

I love being productive. As far back as I can remember, my method for proving my worth has been to always be doing something. My way of gaining a sense of belonging has been to always have something to show for my efforts. I've never been popular, but by golly, I've been necessary, and to remain necessary has required constant productivity. For too long, I have mistakenly believed nonstop fruitfulness to be a sign of spiritual health. And I've feared that fruitlessness must mean I'm spiritually dead.

This fear has driven me to try to force myself to produce more fruit. I've said yes to commitments I knew I wouldn't have the bandwidth to follow through on. I've let myself be distracted from necessary projects by the tyranny of the urgent. I've slid relationships to the back burner, diverting my time and energy to activities that are quickly checked off a to-do list.

And while I've tried to produce, I've fretted about my lack of fruit. *Will she be hurt if I say no this time? What if they find someone better and never ask me again? How will I keep people from assuming I'm—gasp—lazy?*

In Psalm 1:3, we see that bearing fruit is good—in season. But a better, more basic sign of health is having leaves that do not wither. This is evidence of the unseen but ultimate sign of health: being planted "by streams of water" for our roots.

The declaration "whatever they do prospers" includes both yielding lots of fruit in season and producing no fruit during off-season. That's right: Being fruitless is considered prospering when we're not "in season." We don't have to produce all the time in order to prosper all the time. This sounds downright heretical for those of us who tend toward being overly focused on fruit. But it's true: After our fruit is harvested, there's a season during which we don't produce fruit.

Does this make you wonder, *How dare I do nothing?* Rest assured that during off-season we don't actually do *nothing*. What we do may be far less visible, but it's just as important.

Fruitfulness is always God's doing. Like the flats of strawberries that simply show up on my front porch, fruits are His gift to us. (Not the other way around.) And off-season is a gift too. God designed the Sabbath to be a weekly foretaste of off-season. A regular reminder that rest is an integral part of His plan. A time to hear directly from Him about the season we're in, whether fruitful or fallow.

When it's not time to bear fruit, it's time to grow deeper roots. Which means taking the time we need to soak in even more of the goodness of the Living Water. This might mean spending blocks of time in slow, lingering Scripture study with a journaling Bible and pack of highlighters. It might mean reading through a neglected stack of books. It might mean setting aside time to practice silence and solitude. It might mean connecting with a spiritual mentor for encouragement and accountability.

It might mean saying "no" to the scheduling conflict that will have you carpooling the kids at dinnertime. It might mean putting down the phone and not following the news for a week. It might mean bowing out of some regular commitments on your calendar for a season. It might mean letting certain people develop some new self-sufficiency skills.

Here's what I'm learning from embracing the gift of off-season: The more I focus on growing deeper roots, the better the fruit will be . . . in His time.

The Next, Most Faith-Filled Step

Respond to this statement: "We don't have to produce all the time in order to prosper all the time." What season does God have you in right now?

_____

_____

_____

_____

_____

_____

_____

_____

Creating Space

Speak

Read the passage aloud three times.

Ponder

Take a moment to let the words silently flow over you.

Now, some questions to ponder:

What does the passage say?

Why is God bringing you this passage now?

Who comes to mind as you read this passage?

What thoughts come to mind as you ponder?

_____

_____

_____

_____

_____

_____

_____

_____

_____

_____

_____

_____

_____

Act

Is there something God wants you to do because of reading this verse today?

_____

_____

_____

_____

Commit

What has God committed to you in this verse? What promises or truths can you make room for in your thinking?

_____

_____

_____

_____

_____

Express

Finally, take a moment to express aloud to God how you think and feel about your time making space for this piece of Scripture.

_____

_____

_____

_____

_____

One Egg too Far

KATHI

Though the righteous fall seven times, they rise again,
but the wicked stumble when calamity strikes.

PROVERBS 24:16

It had been a rough season for our family. Between aging parents, financial struggles, moving, and setting up a new business, my husband, Roger, and I were burned out, as in, crispy like bacon that had been left in the oven ten minutes too long. Burned. But the hits, they just kept on coming. More stress. More drama. More of everything I didn't need—or want.

As I became more and more overwhelmed with all that was going on in our life, I kept cutting things out to make room for all the tasks that had to get done. Exercise was the first thing to go (funny, it usually is), and then cooking at home gave way to living off a variety of fast-food options. For us, Tuesdays weren't just about tacos. It became Taco Bell Tuesday. Not only was it fast food . . . it wasn't even good fast food.

Sleep was sacrificed and replaced with copious amounts of caffeine in all its forms (coffee, Diet Coke, and then more coffee). And eventually, my time with God fell off my to-do list with a *thunk*.

(But don't you worry. I was all caught up on *Gilmore Girl* reruns.)

It's truly amazing how long we can go, even at our most overwhelmed, inching along, relying on our own strength to get us through the days. I held it together for not weeks, but months. I was pretty impressed at how much capacity I had developed to take on so much hard stuff without a breakdown or even tears.

But then, one day, it all came crashing down.

Or at least the carton of eggs did.

I'd decided what we needed that Saturday morning, after a long, tension-filled week, was a batch of pancakes. Some homemade, add-a-touch-of-vanilla-to-die-for pancakes. I gathered all the ingredients only to drop the very last eggs in the house. You know—the ones I needed to make the homemade, add-a-touch-of-vanilla to-die-for pancakes.

And that's when I lost it. Hard.

I sat on the kitchen floor right next to those useless eggs and cried. And not just a tear, but a wave of messy, dripping, snotty tears that not only frightened my husband but made the dog hide behind the couch, shaking in fear because, obviously, Mom had completely lost her mind.

You know your emotions have gotten the best of you when you realize you've scared the dog.

For months, and sometimes years, I had been living in what many people would consider overwhelming circumstances, but all that time I was at peace because I wasn't handling the circumstances alone. I was relying on God daily. Talking to God daily. In His Word daily.

But when I got to the place of feeling so overwrought that I gave up on not only reading God's Word, but also actually talking to God on the regular—you know, the source of my strength and stability—I was only able to fake the okay for a while.

It didn't last for long, the disconnect from God. But my goal is to get to a place that when I am completely overwhelmed, God is my first thought, and not my last. So often in our overwhelm, our brain tells us to run to God, but our instincts tell us to catch up on the latest Netflix series and clean out all those snack bags that have just a few chips, crackers, and cookies in them . . . in the name of getting organized, of course.

If you, too, need help getting off the kitchen floor, it's time to reach out to God again and ask for help. No fancy prayers. Nothing too spiritual. In fact, my favorite prayer is one word: *Help.* God will not leave you down on the linoleum. It's His greatest desire to see you get up once again and lean on Him. You were not meant to stand alone during the hardest times of your life. (Or sit on the floor for very long either . . .)

Some practical things you can do:

1. Pick up your Bible and start reading in John. When I need to, once again, understand God's love for me, John is a great place to hang out.

2. Listen to your favorite worship music. I have a go-to

playlist of worship music of God's deep love for me. And if you don't have one, start brainstorming some songs that have ministered to you in the past and gather them all in one place. Even while you're having to get other things done—doing dishes, running errands, walking on the treadmill—you can soak in God's deep ministering love for you.

3. And ask a friend if you can hold each other accountable to daily Bible reading. Start with five minutes—or one. Just start. It doesn't matter. (This is an area where shooting low is acceptable.) If you miss a day—hey, it happens to all of us—lovingly and gently remind yourself it's okay and start again. And sometimes, again. The gift of allowing yourself to start again is a beautiful thing.

The Next, Most Faith-Filled Step

If you've been at the place of being too overwhelmed to reach out to God, understand that you're not alone. God is with you in your overwhelm, and you don't need to bear it alone. Even when we're avoiding God, He is pursuing us. Know you are not alone.

One thing I've done that has helped me tremendously is to set an alarm on my phone for three times a day to stop and check in with God. It's amazing how many of those bells go off after I've just been wrestling with a problem or trying to figure things out on my own. The bells go off, and I'm reminded I'm not alone. All I need to do is whisper my one-word prayer, "Help!" and the feeling of having to bear it all on my own is instantly lifted.

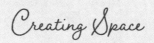

Creating Space

Speak

Read the passage aloud three times.

Ponder

Take a moment to let the words silently flow over you.

Now, some questions to ponder:

What does the passage say?

Why is God bringing you this passage now?

Who comes to mind as you read this passage?

What thoughts come to mind as you ponder?

_____

_____

_____

_____

_____

_____

_____

_____

_____

_____

_____

_____

_____

_____

Act

Is there something God wants you to do because of reading this verse today?

_____

_____

_____

_____

Commit

What has God committed to you in this verse? What promises or truths can you make room for in your thinking?

_____

_____

_____

_____

Express

Finally, take a moment to express aloud to God how you think and feel about your time making space for this piece of Scripture.

_____

_____

_____

_____

_____

Corrosion

CHERI

Get rid of all bitterness, rage and anger, brawling and slander, along with every form of malice. Be kind and compassionate to one another, forgiving each other, just as in Christ God forgave you.

EPHESIANS 4:31-32

One thing that surprised me when we moved from the desert to the coast was the corrosive effect of ocean air.

At first, I thought I was imagining tiny white flecks on my blue sedan. When I looked closer and saw the spots were real, I dismissed them. *They'll come off the next time I drive through a car wash.*

When the white specks remained, I told myself, *They just need a bit of elbow grease.*

But after filling a bucket with soapy water and grabbing a sponge, I discovered that the white spots weren't foreign particles that had settled on my car. They were tiny pits in the protective coating, as if tiny bugs were eating into it.

Only the problem wasn't bugs. The culprit was salt: the unseen but ever-present sodium chloride in ocean air. Because my car was parked outdoors, it was under constant attack from this invisible process of corrosion. Especially on foggy days, when a white shroud of salty mist descended over my car, wreaking further destruction.

Fortunately, a simple solution was available. All I needed to do was take my car to an auto body shop and have a mechanic buff away the corroded spots and apply a new protective coating.

But I didn't have time. Once the school year begins, there are only two times I get anything major accomplished (other than teaching): Christmas break and summer vacation. And I first noticed the white spots on my car in early January.

Six months later, when I finally took my car in, my heart sank as my service representative began speaking in an extra-kind voice. "I'm so sorry, Mrs. Gregory. If you'd brought the car in when you first noticed the problem, it would have been an easy fix. But the corrosion has gone through the protective coating and into the metal. You have a rust issue now."

It's not just my car. My heart, too, is susceptible—to the corrosive effects of bitterness. The hundreds of dollars it takes to halt the progression of rust in a car are nothing compared to the enormous cost of allowing bitterness to fester unchecked in our hearts.

Oh, we can minimize and even gloss over the deterioration for a while.

It's not that bad.

I'll just smile, and we'll move on.

As long as they're happy, I'll be fine.

Truth be told, I spent years feeling secretly smug that while other people might struggle with all the negative emotions listed in Ephesians 4:31, they weren't an issue for me. Not in the least. Pride blinded me to the little white specks of bitterness building up.

My sarcastic remarks were just meant to be humorous . . . not hurtful. My recitations of prior offenses were simply evidence of my good memory . . . not grudge-holding. My subtle withdrawal of affection was purely coincidental . . . not vindictive.

For those of us who take pride in being cooperative and conciliatory, recognizing the dark side of our people-pleasing tendencies can be a slow process. But there comes a time when denial is no longer an option. At some point, our "kind and compassionate" veneer gets worn thin, exposing the rust of "bitterness, rage and anger, brawling and slander, along with every form of malice" within our heart.

After all I've done for them . . .

What makes them think they can treat me like this?

I don't get mad . . . I get even.

Only God can restore our rusted-out hearts.

The longer we delay going to Him, the more damage there will be. Sadly, due to my own stubborn pride, I've had some relationships disintegrate beyond repair. I've come to see the little white specks of bitterness as huge red flags that signal,

"Forgiveness needed NOW!" As we receive His forgiveness, He removes our built-up bitterness with His love and reseals our hearts with His grace.

Then—and only then—can we be kind and compassionate and forgive one another.

The Next, Most Faith-Filled Step

Where do you notice the white specks of bitterness in your heart?

_____

_____

_____

_____

Which relationship is being most impacted, and how?

_____

_____

_____

_____

For what is forgiveness needed?

_____

_____

_____

_____

Creating Space

Speak

Read the passage aloud three times.

Ponder

Take a moment to let the words silently flow over you.

Now, some questions to ponder:

    What does the passage say?

    Why is God bringing you this passage now?

    Who comes to mind as you read this passage?

    What thoughts come to mind as you ponder?

_____

_____

_____

_____

_____

_____

_____

_____

_____

_____

_____

_____

Act

Is there something God wants you to do because of reading this verse today?

_____

_____

_____

_____

Commit

What has God committed to you in this verse? What promises or truths can you make room for in your thinking?

_____

_____

_____

_____

_____

Express

Finally, take a moment to express aloud to God how you think and feel about your time making space for this piece of Scripture.

_____

_____

_____

_____

_____

Chopping Wood

KATHI

*Do not worry about tomorrow, for tomorrow
will worry about itself. Each day has
enough trouble of its own.*

MATTHEW 6:34

We may be the only people in the modern world who know-
ingly bought a house without heating or air-conditioning.
When we questioned how the previous owners heated their house
in the winter, they pointed to the woodshed across the field, and I
realized our lives were about to change dramatically.

Now, every year, our plan is to spend the spring, summer,
and fall chopping wood, so by the time winter rolls around with
her cold nights and darker days, we have stockpiled enough cut
logs to see us through until at least April of the following year.

And that's a great plan—until you realize there's so much
that needs to be done today. As in, right this instant, missy. Including (but not limited to) working our full-time jobs, getting
dinner on the table, keeping on top of cleaning and repairing
the house, paying bills, taking care of all the animals, laundry,
gardening, and more. Add onto all of that trying to prepare

for winter, which is still months off, feels impossible and overwhelming and just not all that urgent.

So instead of cutting wood, we would just spend our time worrying about not having wood.

Have you done that? Spent your energy worrying about not doing something instead of doing the thing you're worried about? When God asks us not to worry about tomorrow, He's not asking us not to care about tomorrow. We all have to care about what is ahead, but what we need not do is borrow the trouble that will surely come.

So how do we take the worry out of tomorrow?

Plan for it. What I finally realized is that I was trying to get too much done each day—and not leaving enough time to plan for my future. But just taking a moment to plan for the next step, even if I don't do anything about that next step, empties the worry out of today. For instance, if Roger and I put on our calendar that we'll take the next free Saturday morning and use that for wood chopping, that's a plan. Every time my brain goes to panic about not having enough wood for winter, I can think about that date circled on the calendar and relax my anxious brain because there's a plan. It's right there on the calendar. No reason to worry. There is a plan.

Trust God for it. God is very clear throughout the Old and New Testaments that worry is on the no-no list. So if God wants us to escape something, He has surely made a way for us to do that.

There are only two ways to increase your trust in God that I have found: by spending time with Him and by relying on Him for the impossible. Now, this can come in a few different ways. When I'm healthy, it's spending time in prayer and His Word, asking Him what His will is, and pursuing it. When I'm not healthy, it's ignoring God, going through a crisis, and calling on Him as a last resort. Both ways work. The first way? Vastly more desirable than the other.

Trust ourselves for it. God has given you a beautiful, curious mind to figure things out. When I become immediately fearful about something coming up in my life—a financial situation, having to learn a new skill, whatever—and that familiar feeling of panic starts to rise up in me, I take a moment and remember that I've been in harder situations and not only has God given me the tools and resources I needed at the time, He's also given me a mind to use to be creative and strategize. I love that when I'm really struggling with a situation, not only do I have the Holy Spirit prompting me, but I also have a God-given mind to think with and use.

Trust the people God has surrounded us with. When I'm in a hard situation, I can feel deeply alone. But when I stop to really think through my resources, one of the biggest is the people God has already surrounded me with.

I have my small crew of friends on a text chain I can call upon at any point for love, laughs, and prayers. I have my husband, who is my constant rock in any situation, and I have my favorite Facebook group that I can go to with any prayer, big or small.

When worry starts to invade your heart and mind, remember all the ways God has already equipped you to face the future with Him.

The Next, Most Faith-Filled Step

One way I like to break down overwhelming tasks is to think, *What is the next, most faith-filled step I can take on this project?* Not the next twenty steps. Not the next big step. What is something I can do in the next five minutes to push this forward? It's a great way to make progress, lessen the guilt, and keep moving forward.

Creating Space

Speak

Read the passage aloud three times.

Ponder

Take a moment to let the words silently flow over you.

Now, some questions to ponder:

> What does the passage say?
>
> Why is God bringing you this passage now?
>
> Who comes to mind as you read this passage?
>
> What thoughts come to mind as you ponder?

_____

_____

_____

_____

_____

_____

_____

_____

_____

_____

_____

_____

_____

Act

Is there something God wants you to do because of reading this verse today?

_____

_____

_____

_____

Commit

What has God committed to you in this verse? What promises or truths can you make room for in your thinking?

_____

_____

_____

_____

_____

Express

Finally, take a moment to express aloud to God how you think and feel about your time making space for this piece of Scripture.

_____

_____

_____

_____

_____

For Freedom

CHERI

It is for freedom that Christ has set us free.
Stand firm, then, and do not let yourselves
be burdened again by a yoke of slavery.

GALATIANS 5:1

Daniel and I had been looking forward to this particular evening all summer. First, dinner with Kathi and Roger Lipp. And then—drumroll—Tim Hawkins in concert!

But as we drove toward San Jose, we could hardly keep our eyes open, let alone muster excitement. Having just returned from an overseas trip, our jetlagged bodies had no idea where we were or what time it was. They just demanded sleep. Now.

"Do you think Kathi and Roger will mind if I rest my eyes on their couch for a few minutes?" Daniel asked.

I hesitated. I knew that Kathi and Roger had made reservations to take us out to dinner. I was afraid of spoiling the perfect evening they'd been planning. But I also knew Daniel needed a nap more than anything. Otherwise, he'd fall asleep in his salad.

Pushing past fear, I texted Kathi: "Daniel's beat. Could he nap on your couch for an hour or so once we get there?"

Meanwhile, Kathi and Roger were in the middle of their own conundrum. They'd committed to taking us out to dinner before a string of unexpected financial challenges. Now, unknown to us, they were in a no-spend summer. Kathi was afraid to go back on her word: They could rationalize charging this one dinner on their credit card, couldn't they?

Because of unexpected traffic, Daniel and I were almost an hour late to the Lipps's. The entire time, I did mental math, calculating Daniel's nap time shrinking and shrinking and finally disappearing. All we had time for was dinner and the Tim Hawkins show. Daniel was going to be a zombie.

So when Kathi welcomed us with the words, "Sorry, guys, but we're eating in tonight," we fell over ourselves assuring her it would be "Fine, just fine, *more* than fine!" (We may or may not have shed actual tears of relief.) Daniel crashed on their comfy couch for two solid hours while Kathi and I recorded a couple of podcasts upstairs.

Then we shared a simple meal of tomato soup, salad, homemade bread, and strawberry shortcake (with fresh whipped cream!). We sat around the very kitchen table where our first coauthored book was born two years prior, talking and listening and talking and listening and talking some more. And then we headed to the Tim Hawkins concert, where we sat together and laughed ourselves silly.

That simple meal was exactly what we needed. And it was

clear evidence of God's transforming power—confirmation that we were set free from the powerful yoke of slavery known as perfectionism.

Oh, I'd still heard an inner voice loudly insisting, "You can't appear ungrateful. You have to drag yourself out to dinner with them, no matter how exhausted you feel." And Kathi's internal monologue had been just as demanding: "You have to take them out to dinner! You promised! What kind of friend doesn't stick to her word?"

If we'd caved to our respective fears of seeming ungrateful or flakey, we would have done things "perfectly" by going out to dinner. And we all would have been miserable, although none of us would have known why. Instead, we acted from a place of freedom. Freedom to stand firm against the burden of perfectionism. Freedom to speak candidly about our needs. Freedom to flex our plans. Freedom to offer and receive grace.

I never ever want to take these freedoms for granted.

Now that I know what it's like to live free, I want to be intentional about standing firm. Not just for my own sake, but also for the people I love.

I used to think the decades I spent enslaved to perfectionism impacted only me. But it's become clear that my friends and family members, too, bore the burden of my invisible yoke. Oh, I regularly insisted "I'm only this hard on myself!" But saying these words aloud didn't make them true . . . or okay.

I'm grateful for a friendship that has helped me learn what "it is for freedom that Christ has set us free" can look like in the practical nitty-gritty of everyday life.

And I want to be the kind of friend who supports others as they, too, stand firm against this particular yoke of slavery. Don't you? This means inviting the Holy Spirit to shine His light onto our expectations and hidden agendas. It means speaking honestly about our own needs and inviting others to do the same. It means learning the skill of flexibility. And putting it into practice. Often.

It means celebrating God's transforming power. And it means grounding our day-to-day decisions in the truth: Christ has set us free!

The Next, Most Faith-Filled Step

Where in your life have you experienced God's transforming power to set you free? What might it look like for you to "stand firm" in this freedom for yourself? What burdens would this release from others?

_____

_____

_____

_____

_____

_____

_____

Creating Space

Speak

Read the passage aloud three times.

Ponder

Take a moment to let the words silently flow over you.

Now, some questions to ponder:

What does the passage say?

Why is God bringing you this passage now?

Who comes to mind as you read this passage?

What thoughts come to mind as you ponder?

_____

_____

_____

_____

_____

_____

_____

_____

_____

_____

_____

_____

_____

Act

Is there something God wants you to do because of reading this verse today?

_____

_____

_____

_____

Commit

What has God committed to you in this verse? What promises or truths can you make room for in your thinking?

_____

_____

_____

_____

Express

Finally, take a moment to express aloud to God how you think and feel about your time making space for this piece of Scripture.

_____

_____

_____

_____

Not Hard Enough

KATHI

Unless the LORD builds the house, they labor in
vain who build it; unless the LORD guards the city,
the watchman stays awake in vain.
It is vain for you to rise up early, to sit up late,
to eat the bread of sorrows; for so He
gives His beloved sleep.

PSALM 127:1-2 NKJV

Yesterday, someone accused me of not working hard enough. Oh, friend! Tell me you think my dog is ugly or you hate the way I decorate my house or you don't like my writing or you've had better chocolate chip cookies than the ones I just served you. (Okay, that's nonsense. No one makes better chocolate chip cookies than I do.) But to tell me I'm not working hard enough? That pushes on every last insecurity I have.

Because, you see, I am recovering from a history of not working hard enough. When I was a kid, I would unload the dishwasher but not unload the silverware. Putting away a pot got a lot of the dishwasher unloaded at once. But a spoon? I was barely making a dent. (I like to see maximum results for the littlest actions.) Better to leave that to someone else whose time was less valuable than the very important schedule of an eleven-year-old.

But when I started going to a church that basically said that working hard and loving God were the same thing, it reinforced what I'd always believed—that hard work and pleasing God were tied together. (If you asked me if that was true, my brain would say no. But if you asked my heart? Absolutely!) And as an adult, I've been proud of my work ethic and the work ethic of my family. It's a good thing to do a good job.

So yesterday . . .

Someone asked me to send them an email, and I did. But it didn't get to them (thank you, spam filter), and this person was mad. And they said I just wasn't trying hard enough. And the accusation cut me. Truly, it did.

Because that accusation took me back to a time before I knew Christ, when I was a child and I acted like a child. Trying to get away with things, trying to get out of things. But I've changed, and I see that as growing in Christ.

And then I go overboard. It goes past keeping my word and brings me back to a place where, on my missions team, I wanted to serve longer than anyone else. Or I wanted to earn more money to give to the homeless shelter than anyone else. Or bring more friends to church on "Friend Sunday" than anyone else. I took on church like I was part of a multilevel marketing scheme where I would get praised for working harder, raising more money, and recruiting more people than anyone else.

You see, it's in my insecurity that I need to know that *you* know that I've worked hard.

It's even that way in my marriage. My husband is a hard worker. (This is one of the things that definitely attracted me to him.) He works hard at his corporate job. He works hard helping me in my business. And he works hard at taking care of our little corner of the mountain—all 33 acres of it.

It's a lot of work, and he works with joy. And when he's done, he rests in the peace and knowledge that he's done a good day's work.

Me? Not so much. I feel like I'm still trying to make up for my lazy eleven-year-old self. Trying to prove to you, and everyone else I know, that I'm no longer that lazy kid shirking work. So I get up early and I work too late to make sure you know I'm carrying my load. And my husband knows.

Here's the problem with that: I'm never able to rest, truly rest, because I always have something to prove. To you. To my husband. To God. To myself. And when it comes down to it, for me, my lack of rest is a lack of trust. I'm not trusting God with my efforts.

When I trust in God—that He has appointed my day and my efforts—I can rest at the end of the day, knowing I've done what I can and the results are up to God. I can trust that I have done my portion. I can trust that God has everything under control. I don't have to wear my anxiety like a badge of honor, proving that I care just as much as everyone else does.

How do I turn this thinking around? One way is by realizing

that one of the holiest acts of worship I can perform is to go to bed at a decent hour. To remind myself that "He gives His beloved sleep."

God cares for me. I am His beloved. And when I'm anxious, tossing and turning over all that is left undone, what I really need to do is to turn that anxiety over to Him who calls me beloved.

If you're an overworker, a prover of the fact that you're working enough, there is hope for you. There is hope for me.

The hope? It's not only in reading God's Word but in believing it.

The hope? It's not only believing God's Word but also believing that it's meant for you.

You and I? We're truly His beloved. And we can rest in that.

The Next, Most Faith-Filled Step

Are you someone who can never rest? I was that person. (I sometimes still am that person.) But then I started to look at rest as *trust*.

Trust that God has not left the situation all up to me.

Trust that God knows my limits.

Trust that God has others He relies on to do His work.

Rest became more than an option. It became an act of worship.

Today, can you schedule in a place of rest? Not if you get everything done. Not if everything is okay. But just because you can trust God with the undone. The not-okayness of it all. Put a reminder on your schedule today of 15 minutes of trust-filled rest.

Creating Space

Speak
Read the passage aloud three times.

Ponder
Take a moment to let the words silently flow over you.

Now, some questions to ponder:

What does the passage say?

Why is God bringing you this passage now?

Who comes to mind as you read this passage?

What thoughts come to mind as you ponder?

_____

_____

_____

_____

_____

_____

_____

_____

_____

_____

_____

_____

_____

Act

Is there something God wants you to do because of reading this verse today?

_____

_____

_____

_____

Commit

What has God committed to you in this verse? What promises or truths can you make room for in your thinking?

_____

_____

_____

_____

_____

Express

Finally, take a moment to express aloud to God how you think and feel about your time making space for this piece of Scripture.

_____

_____

_____

_____

_____

Motion and Direction

CHERI

Whether you turn to the right or to the left,
your ears will hear a voice behind you,
saying, "This is the way; walk in it."

ISAIAH 30:21

ravel east to Santa Cruz Avenue," my GPS cheerfully directs me.

"You are useless!" I respond, gesturing toward the cars around me. "I'm sitting in a parking lot. How am I supposed to 'Travel east to Santa Cruz Avenue' when I don't know which way is east and have no clue where Santa Cruz Avenue is?"

Trying to get my bearings, I enlarge the map on my cell phone screen. But it's no use. I have no idea which way to go.

For a moment, I struggle. Back in my perfectionism days, "I don't know the right way" was the worst feeling in the world. Now, by God's grace, I'm not nearly as hard on myself for mistakes as I used to be. I'm willing to explore, experiment, try, and—*gasp*—fail.

And I certainly don't want to sit here all day. So I start my car, pull out of my parking spot, and start to drive.

In what direction? I have no clue.

Within seconds, my GPS chirps, "In .2 miles, turn right onto Santa Cruz Avenue." I smile and accelerate. This I can do.

As I stop at the light and signal my turn, I recall something a friend said during a recent discussion about spiritual growth: "I think we need to be in motion to get more direction." This principle has certainly proved true for me today. But taking action when I lack direction is still a very new thing for me.

You see, I've always been a planner. Not the "Oh good— someone who knows how to turn a great idea into an even better reality" kind of planner. But the "Oh no—someone who insists on mapping out every possible worst-case scenario" kind of planner. I spent the first four decades of my life convinced that the only justification for taking action was possession of the perfect plan.

I longed to learn to take action sooner, to step out in faith more often. Doing nothing felt safer than risking the wrong thing, but it left me sitting in the parking lot of life.

Maybe you've been there too—awaiting clear direction before taking any action. But when we read Bible stories of the people who demonstrated great faith in God, it's clear that He never gave them divine roadmaps for their lives. Instead, He gave Himself.

To Abram, God said, "Go . . . to the land *I* will show you" (Genesis 12:1).

Simon Peter and Andrew heard Jesus say, "Come, follow *me*" (Matthew 4:19).

"This is the way; walk in it" is the voice of Israel's Shepherd calling out to His lost sheep. We, too, can hear our Good Shepherd's voice behind us as He guards and guides us. He watches where we're going, and often it's when we come to a fork in the road that we'll get His next direction.

Unfortunately, like the children of Israel, I can be obstinate. I can't tell you how many times I've rationalized: *I'm a big picture kinda gal. Before I do anything, I must first plan everything.* Over the years, I made so many big, beautiful plans. I planned the weekly lessons for a girls' Bible study in our home. I planned the menus and shopping lists for meals to take to families in crisis. I planned service projects for our family to participate in during holiday breaks.

However, my grand plans never became anything other than plans. Looking back, I can see how much time and energy I spent "going through the motions" rather than setting myself in motion. God kept calling me to put down my pens and Post-it Notes and get going, but I was parked in my plans.

Then, I heard Kathi share the analogy of a person who "is always saddling up but never getting on the horse to ride," and realized she was describing me to a T! I started noticing how much perfectionism was tangled up in all my planning. And I started recognizing that whenever God called me to "walk," anything other than action was willful disobedience on my part.

Even planning.

So I started putting myself in motion. After so many years of hiding behind my plans, it was a bit scary leaving life's parking lot, not knowing for sure which way to go. But mostly, it was exciting to take action, listening for God's direction. And in the years since, I've found that when we're walking in faith, one thing really does lead to another. Saying *yes* to God's promptings has opened up new opportunities, put me in place to begin new relationships, and led me down a path I would never have envisioned.

Your case will look different from mine, of course. But the same principle applies to each one of us. Get in motion to get more direction.

The Next, Most Faith-Filled Step

In what area of your life are you "parked"? Perhaps even hiding behind your plans? What is one way you can get yourself in motion so you can get God's next direction?

_____

_____

_____

_____

_____

_____

_____

_____

Creating Space

Speak

Read the passage aloud three times.

Ponder

Take a moment to let the words silently flow over you.

Now, some questions to ponder:

What does the passage say?

Why is God bringing you this passage now?

Who comes to mind as you read this passage?

What thoughts come to mind as you ponder?

_____

_____

_____

_____

_____

_____

_____

_____

_____

_____

_____

_____

_____

Act

Is there something God wants you to do because of reading this verse today?

_____

_____

_____

_____

Commit

What has God committed to you in this verse? What promises or truths can you make room for in your thinking?

_____

_____

_____

_____

_____

Express

Finally, take a moment to express aloud to God how you think and feel about your time making space for this piece of Scripture.

_____

_____

_____

_____

_____

Fire Starting

KATHI

*Be anxious for nothing, but in everything by prayer
and supplication, with thanksgiving, let your requests
be made known to God; and the peace of God, which
surpasses all understanding, will guard your
hearts and minds through Christ Jesus.*

PHILIPPIANS 4:6-7 NKJV

Each morning from late fall to early spring is the same: Wake up, hit Go on the coffeepot, let the dog out, and build a fire. For us, building a fire isn't an exercise in ambiance. We don't have central heating in our house, so our fireplace is our primary means of staying warm during the chillier months.

And when it comes to building that fire? Well, that's where things get interesting.

Since I'm the early riser in our relationship, I have two choices on cold mornings: attempt to build a fire, or wear three sweatshirts and gloves for my morning writing until Roger gets up and can put his lumberjack skills to use.

I gamble on the fire more often than not.

There are some mornings when I can throw three logs together, tuck in a little kindling, and boom, the fire is lit. That's about 5 percent of the time. The other 95 percent of the time? It takes a combination of time, patience, and dumb luck to get past anything beyond a smolder.

Most mornings, lighting a fire takes me more than a couple of tries. (I'm getting better, but it is a process.) So many mornings, I spend a lot of my early minutes lighting, adjusting, and praying the fire will start. And many times, I just can't get it going.

At that point in the process, I have three options:

1. *Keep working.* Sometimes, I just need to keep working to get the fire going. Maybe I need to find some smaller pieces of kindling or light that kindling in a different place. Most of the time, it's the logs that need to be rearranged in a way that's more conducive to starting the fire—and keeping it going. *There are times when I just need to keep working harder.*

2. *Step away.* There are mornings when I just need to step away from the fire. This has happened more times than I care to admit. Those days, I've spent a good chunk of my day fussing over the fire. I've done all the things, but nothing seems to work. Nothing at all. So I give up, ignoring Moose the dog's judgmental stare, and instead, step away, bundle up, and head outside to take care of the chickens. Funny thing is, when I come back inside and open the fireplace door, the logs are at full blaze. *There are times when I need to meddle less and just step away.*

3. *Turn it over to someone else.* There are some mornings when, for me, the fire isn't going to happen. I want to keep work-

ing at it. (It's a pride thing.) I don't need anyone else to take over the fire. I'm fine. No, really, I'm fine. But *there are times when I need to ask someone else to take on the work.*

Recently, life got stressful. My husband got sick while his mother was on hospice a continent away. I went to work administering all the home remedies to help Roger and did everything I could to keep him comfortable while also staying in touch with family to check on his mom. I kept working at all the things, hoping Roger would improve. Because *sometimes, we do need to keep working on it.* There are situations that lead us to worry, but God calls us to both pray about the situation and keep at it.

When Roger didn't improve, it became clear he needed medical care, which meant a middle-of-the-night drive down the mountain to the hospital. Where, because of the pandemic protocol, I spent the first night of his hospital stay in my Jeep in the parking structure of the emergency wing of the hospital. I waited on word from the doctors. Finally, Roger texted me saying, "They don't know what's wrong, but they're keeping me."

I literally had to step away, leave my husband at a hospital I'd never even seen the inside of, and go home. *Sometimes, we need to surrender and step away.*

When my efforts didn't help Roger improve, and when it became clear we could do nothing to help Roger's mom because of our circumstances, I had to turn care for both Roger and his mom over to others—medical professionals for Roger and other family members for Roger's mom. But more than that, I had to turn my worry over to someone else too—Jesus. *Sometimes, we need to turn it all over to someone else.* And that takes faith.

The Gospel of Mark tells a story about faith like that.

> A few days later, when Jesus again entered Capernaum, the people heard that he had come home. They gathered in such large numbers that there was no room left, not even outside the door, and he preached the word to them. Some men came, bringing to him a paralyzed man, carried by four of them. Since they could not get him to Jesus because of the crowd, they made an opening in the roof above Jesus by digging through it and then lowered the mat the man was lying on. When Jesus saw their faith, he said to the paralyzed man, "Son, your sins are forgiven" (Mark 2:1-5).

The part of those verses that stick out to me is this: "When Jesus saw their faith . . ." It was the faith of the four men who were carrying their friend that caused Jesus to heal him. Sometimes, we are so overwhelmed, hurt, crushed, and bruised that our prayers seem ineffectual and weak. At those points, as an act of faith, we call in reinforcements by asking friends if they will share the burden with us. Sharing the burden keeps us from giving up.

Whether we are in the *working harder* stage or the *asking for help* stage, we need to do the most loving thing for ourselves and be in the *trusting God with every detail* stage. It's only when we know that earthly efforts are under the umbrella of a loving God that we can truly rest in not only who He is but also how we're moving forward.

The Next, Most Faith-Filled Step

When I'm in that spot of worry and anxiety, my brain can go to a million different places. It is truly a relief to go through this list of three options and see what I need to do. Do I need to . . .

1. keep working,
2. step away, or
3. turn it over to someone else?

Think about a current circumstance that has more anxiety around it than you'd like. Which one of those three steps do you need to employ? What is that next, most faith-filled step you need to take?

_____

_____

_____

_____

_____

Creating Space

Speak

Read the passage aloud three times.

Ponder

Take a moment to let the words silently flow over you.

Now, some questions to ponder:

What does the passage say?

Why is God bringing you this passage now?

Who comes to mind as you read this passage?

What thoughts come to mind as you ponder?

_____

_____

_____

_____

_____

_____

_____

_____

_____

_____

_____

_____

Act

Is there something God wants you to do because of reading this verse today?

_____

_____

_____

_____

Commit

What has God committed to you in this verse? What promises or truths can you make room for in your thinking?

_____

_____

_____

_____

Express

Finally, take a moment to express aloud to God how you think and feel about your time making space for this piece of Scripture.

_____

_____

_____

_____

_____

Stay in the Water

CHERI

I keep my eyes always on the LORD.
With him at my right hand, I will not be shaken.
Therefore my heart is glad and my tongue rejoices;
my body also will rest secure.

PSALM 16:8-9

I *want out of the water.*

I'm bobbing in the ocean, with angry storm clouds above and choppy waves all around. My husband, who has just disappeared from view, is an enthusiastic multi-certified Master Diver. I've only just taken the "Resort SCUBA" class.

I put my face under for a moment, and to my horror I can see absolutely nothing. In the practice pool this morning, I could see the sides and the bottom. Here, I see nothing but murky green water.

I *want out of the water.*

My mask fogs with tears I'm fighting to restrain. I can't remember ever feeling this level of sheer terror. The dive master reaches for my hand, but I swim away.

"What's wrong, lady?" he asks. "What are you afraid of?

Please come down the rope!"

I shake my head and point toward the boat, where I can climb on board, strip off my mask, fins, tank, buoyancy control device, and eventually tell Daniel, "This just isn't for me."

"Come." The dive master gently takes my hand and guides me back toward the rope. "I will be your angel today."

I am not putting my head back under. I am not going down there. I want out of the water. Out, out, out, out, OUT!

But somehow, I find myself a few inches under, face-to-face with my dive master. He motions for me to breathe in. Instinctively, I obey. My hands move a few inches further down the rope, and I breathe out. I fall into an intentional rhythm. Move a few inches: breathe in. Move a few more inches: breathe out. All the way down the rope, I take in and let out air the way I've been taught.

Suddenly, Daniel materializes, and then I can see the bottom.

Standing on the ocean floor, I look around, taking in wondrous surroundings. I am in an unfathomably beautiful world, a glorious universe set apart. For years, Daniel has tried to tell me, tried to explain why he loves to dive. But not until now do I understand.

I do not want out of the water. I may never get out of the water again.

Later, back on dry land, I think about how close I came to

getting out. I would have been so sure I'd made the right choice, but I would have been so very wrong.

Twenty years later, I still remember the difference it made to lock eyes with my dive master and trust him to take me by the hand. Now, when the angry storm clouds and choppy waves of life's challenges surround me, David's words in Psalm 16:8-9 mirror the pivotal lessons I learned that day.

1. *I keep my eyes always on the Lord.* When I focus on my difficult circumstances, the most natural reaction is to feel overwhelmed, even panicky. Especially if I try to dive in all by myself! It takes practice to keep my eyes always on the Lord. Whatever the situation, I can recite, "I keep my eyes always on the LORD."

Rough day at work? "I keep my eyes always on the LORD."

Relational conflict? "I keep my eyes always on the LORD."

Financial challenge? "I keep my eyes always on the LORD."

Not in a cliché sort of way. But as an intentional choice to look away from the cause of our fear and focus on the Source of our faith.

2. *With Him at my right hand, I will not be shaken.* On my own, I'm neither courageous nor resilient; I'm a staller-outer and quitter. But God's power overrides my natural weaknesses, giving me His strength to accomplish hard things I could never do by myself.

Regardless of what we're facing, we can take this to heart: "With him at my right hand, I will not be shaken." Internalize these words by squeezing your right hand in acknowledgement of God's intimate presence and holding your left palm open in front of you in acknowledgement of His promised power.

Lost job? "With him at my right hand, I will not be shaken" (right hand, left palm).

Unexpected diagnosis? "With him at my right hand, I will not be shaken" (right hand, left palm).

Broken relationship? "With him at my right hand, I will not be shaken" (right hand, left palm).

3. *My heart is glad and my tongue rejoices.* Because I'm problem-prone, I know it's vital for me to intentionally notice God's goodness throughout each day. While I do keep a written gratitude journal, I also need to praise God spontaneously.

Wherever we are, we can send up a silent prayer: "My heart is glad and my tongue rejoices" when we see evidence of God's transforming power in our lives.

Birds singing? "My heart is glad and my tongue rejoices."

Technicolor sunset? "My heart is glad and my tongue rejoices."

Delectable flavors? "My heart is glad and my tongue rejoices."

4. *My body also will rest secure.* As someone who lives with hypervigilance—my body is constantly on high alert—I find great comfort in this line. As we move and tend and rest our bodies, we can express confidence that God is with us and watching over us.

Taking a walk? "My body also will rest secure."

Getting a massage? "My body also will rest secure."

Settling down for a nap? "My body also will rest secure."

Lock eyes with your Dive Master and trust Him to take you by the hand.

The Next, Most Faith-Filled Step

The next time the angry storm clouds and choppy waves of life's challenges surround you, try praying through Psalm 16:8-9 as a breath prayer:

(Breathe in:)	I keep my eyes
(Breathe out:)	always on the LORD.
(Breathe in:)	With him at my right hand,
(Breathe out:)	I will not be shaken.
(Breathe in:)	Therefore my heart is glad
(Breathe out:)	and my tongue rejoices;
(Breathe in:)	my body also
(Breathe out:)	will rest secure.

Creating Space

Speak

Read the passage aloud three times.

Ponder

Take a moment to let the words silently flow over you.

Now, some questions to ponder:

    What does the passage say?

    Why is God bringing you this passage now?

    Who comes to mind as you read this passage?

    What thoughts come to mind as you ponder?

_____

_____

_____

_____

_____

_____

_____

_____

_____

_____

_____

_____

Act

Is there something God wants you to do because of reading this verse today?

_____

_____

_____

_____

Commit

What has God committed to you in this verse? What promises or truths can you make room for in your thinking?

_____

_____

_____

_____

_____

Express

Finally, take a moment to express aloud to God how you think and feel about your time making space for this piece of Scripture.

_____

_____

_____

_____

_____

KATHI

The Spirit God gave us does not make us timid,
but gives us power, love and self-discipline.

2 TIMOTHY 1:7

Maybe it's when I get on the scale. You know, with my fingers shielding my eyes and then quickly peeking at the number that so rudely pops on the display. Or when I see my walking shoes in the closet, where they have lived for the past two weeks, never seeing the light of day. Maybe it's when I walk into my laundry room and see the piles (plural) of clothes I swore I was going to get to this week. Or when I pick up a stack of mail that has been sitting on my counter, silently shaming me for a month, only to find my even more-neglected Bible sitting under it.

That's when the accusations start to come . . .

Loser.

Hopeless.

Pathetic.

These are just a few of the many words that I've used to

describe myself when, once again, I failed at something I set my mind to. Whether it's losing weight, reading my Bible, avoiding the drive-thru, or decluttering my home once and for all, I've tried and failed more times than even I'm willing to count. (Another thing I've given up on. *Sigh . . .*)

And I'm guessing I'm not alone in this kind of destructive self-talk. I'd never say these words aloud, but they scream inside my head louder than any other voices in my head. Isn't it crazy that we say things to ourselves we would never even say to that bully (the awful guy at work or the meanie mom at our kid's school) because we're so much more compassionate to the worst people around us than we are to ourselves?

And here's the crazy thing: It's sometimes over the smallest thing. I can be just as cruel to myself for absently popping a donut hole into my mouth as I would be if I binge ate through my local Krispy Creme. Because, in my world, black and white is just that. One step towards the dark and I'm a complete failure. And yes, this is an exhausting way to live.

And if I talk to myself like that once . . . well, I can recover. But if I allow it to build into a mixtape of self-awfulness playing on repeat? I start to believe those things to the very cells of my being.

When we're in that place of being defeated and dejected, how do we summon the energy to keep on going? When I'm looking at making a change in my life, my mind immediately goes to all those times I tried to change before and failed. I start to think, "What will be different this time? You're just doomed for more failure."

But here's what I've learned about trying and failing: You learn something new with each attempt. You become better and stronger. And more importantly, you learn something new about God—about His love and His mercy—every time you try and it doesn't come out the way you intended.

And, ultimately, you learn that God is more powerful in your life than you've previously given Him credit for.

And look at those three things God promises us . . .

Power.

Love.

Self-discipline.

Whoa! Those three attributes aren't promised only to other people. They're promised to you as a child of God.

But here's the one part of that verse I've skipped over in the past: "The Spirit God gave us does not make us timid." How does *timid* show up in my life?

I'm too timid to believe I can change.

I'm too timid to think God can use me in any real and significant way.

I'm too timid to allow myself to believe I can have the self-discipline to make anything different happen.

If you talk to other women, and I mean really talk, you'll

realize you're truly not alone in all this loneliness of giving up. Yes, I know it seems like everyone around you is scaling new mountains, starting new diets, completing new projects, and just winning all over the place. What you don't see are the women who are quietly falling, picking themselves up, and trusting God for another day.

Find those women.

Hang out with those women.

Be with the people who are not only showing you their mountaintop experiences but also their pits. Women who are triumphing after they've tripped up are the women who will inspire you the most and help you keep going.

And most importantly, surround yourself with the ones who are talking about how God met them on the mountaintop *and* when they were stuck in the ditch and felt all alone, hopeless, ready to give up. Spend time with those who share how God reached down into that pit and pulled them out, placing their feet on solid ground.

We need to hear the stories of those who have failed over and over again, those God then met with power, love, and self-control. The women who decided once and for all they were no longer going to let their timid thoughts run their days and nights. Those who, instead, became completely sold out to the God who loves them and gives them what they need—power, love, and self-discipline—to change their lives.

The Next, Most Faith-Filled Step

Identify a woman in your life who has tried, failed, and then gotten up again. Send her a note (or a text, or a Facebook message, or even an old-fashioned email) and call out in her the resolve you want to see in yourself.

Then, ask God to give you a little more resolve today than you had yesterday.

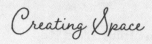

Creating Space

Speak

Read the passage aloud three times.

Ponder

Take a moment to let the words silently flow over you.

Now, some questions to ponder:

    What does the passage say?

    Why is God bringing you this passage now?

    Who comes to mind as you read this passage?

    What thoughts come to mind as you ponder?

_____

_____

_____

_____

_____

_____

_____

_____

_____

_____

_____

_____

Act

Is there something God wants you to do because of reading this verse today?

_____

_____

_____

_____

Commit

What has God committed to you in this verse? What promises or truths can you make room for in your thinking?

_____

_____

_____

_____

_____

Express

Finally, take a moment to express aloud to God how you think and feel about your time making space for this piece of Scripture.

_____

_____

_____

_____

_____

CHERI

Your word is a lamp for my feet,
a light on my path.

PSALM 119:105

When my friend Amy came to visit for a week, I was eager to pull out all the stops as a hostess-with-the-mostest. But several days into what we dubbed the "Coffee and Carbs Tour of the Central California Coast," Amy sweetly suggested we engage in some actual exercise.

"How about kayaking?" I asked.

"Sounds fun!" she replied.

Thirty minutes later, we were buckling on neon-yellow life vests, signing waivers, and waiting for the required "how to kayak without drowning or being swept out to open sea" video to finish.

Yeah, yeah, yeah, I thought. *I've been kayaking all my life. Let's go!*

Finally, we climbed into our kayaks, Amy cheering as neither one of us capsized. "Woo-hoo! Off to a great start!"

We spent a few minutes paddling around the little marina in front of the kayak rental shop, gaining our balance and finding our rhythm as we alternated strokes. Soon, we headed to the inlet. To our right was the Pacific Ocean, to the left, Elkhorn Slough. We steered our tiny crafts up the slough.

And began to paddle with all our might. At first, it felt good to break a sweat. Dip left, pull hard. Dip right, pull hard. Over and over and over again. I leaned forward, giving it my all. Out of the corner of my eye, I could see that Amy was doing the same. In no time at all, we'd be a mile or so up Elkhorn Slough, snapping photos of a beautiful cove with sea otters swimming around us and seals lounging on the shores.

When I was sure we were halfway there, I paused for a breather. But as I looked around to enjoy the changing scenery, I was in for a shock: It was as if we'd been sitting still. Despite all the energy we'd expended, we'd made no measurable progress. And now that I'd stopped paddling, I could feel the current pulling my little craft backwards, toward the open sea.

"I think the tide is going out!" Amy called out. My heart sank as the truth landed. *The tide. Of course. I should have checked the tide!*

It wasn't just an ordinary tide, we later learned. It was a "king tide"—the extra high tide that comes with a full moon.

I would have known this if I'd only taken the time to check the tide tables. It wouldn't have been hard. Unlike the olden days, when tide tables were printed in an almanac, all the information I needed to illuminate my decision-making was mere mouse clicks away. Instead, I acted on blind impulse, which got me nowhere. Literally.

Once Amy and I recognized the futility of our situation, we turned around and headed back to the marina. We laughed at ourselves the whole drive home, dismissing our sore muscles as a small price to pay for the joy of spontaneity. The day certainly wasn't a disaster, but there was an element of disappointment. Whenever I think back to our ill-fated kayaking trip, I can't help but imagine the pictures we'd have . . . *if I'd only taken the time to check the tide tables.*

We missed out.

In my everyday life, I miss out when I don't take the time to check God's "tide tables"—a book full of divine inspiration to illuminate my decision-making. But when that still small voice reminds me to go to God's Word first, I get impatient. Too often, my gut reaction is *Yeah, yeah, yeah. I've been reading my Bible all my life. Let's go!* When I'm in such a rush that my Bible gathers dust, I experience avoidable disappointment. Just as Amy and I only got partway to the beautiful cove with sea otters and seals, my day-to-day spontaneity typically fizzles and falls short.

The real problem with my spontaneity is that it hides a deeper heart issue: self-sufficiency. Amy and I didn't just miss out on some memorable marine life photos. We missed out on paddling with the tide instead of against it. We missed out on having a power immeasurably greater than ourselves carry us forward to our destination. In the same way, blind self-sufficiency means I miss out on hearing God's guidance and experiencing His power in my day-to-day life.

The antidote to self-sufficiency is surrender—yielding leadership of my life to the One who created me. After all, He knows me better than I know myself . . . and He knows what's best for me. I want to live with the same intimate confidence in God the psalmist expresses in Psalm 119:105: "Your word is a lamp for my feet, a light on my path." I want checking God's "tide tables" to be my first instinct, not an afterthought that occurs to me only when my spontaneous plans are going nowhere. I want each time I open my Bible to be an intentional choice to surrender my plans to God.

When you open your Bible before jumping into action, you'll find that God's Word is an ever-lit lamp, a light that's always shining. Check His "tide tables" and receive His loving guidance. Experience His power moving you forward to His plans for you. When you start each new venture in the light of God's Word, you'll never miss out on Him.

The Next, Most Faith-Filled Step

When you feel like you're paddling for all you're worth but getting nowhere, and possibly even being pulled out to sea, let this simple question serve as a helpful heart-check: Have you taken time to check the tide tables?

Creating Space

Speak

Read the passage aloud three times.

Ponder

Take a moment to let the words silently flow over you.

Now, some questions to ponder:

    What does the passage say?

    Why is God bringing you this passage now?

    Who comes to mind as you read this passage?

    What thoughts come to mind as you ponder?

_____

_____

_____

_____

_____

_____

_____

_____

_____

_____

_____

_____

_____

Act

Is there something God wants you to do because of reading this verse today?

_____

_____

_____

_____

Commit

What has God committed to you in this verse? What promises or truths can you make room for in your thinking?

_____

_____

_____

_____

Express

Finally, take a moment to express aloud to God how you think and feel about your time making space for this piece of Scripture.

_____

_____

_____

_____

_____

How Does Your Garden Grow?

KATHI

Consider it pure joy, my brothers and sisters, whenever you face trials of many kinds, because you know that the testing of your faith produces perseverance. Let perseverance finish its work so that you may be mature and complete, not lacking anything.

JAMES 1:2-4

One of the things I'm learning about living in the mountains is that rules that apply to everyone else don't always apply up here.

In baking, everything takes longer and needs to be at a higher temperature. (You know those "high altitude" instructions on the back of the cake box? Those were written for me.)

In the city, I would stay up until 11:00 at night working on projects and watching reruns of *Madam Secretary* but then would toss and turn all night and never get enough sleep. Here in the mountains, if I want to get extra work done, it'd better be at 5:30 in the morning because at 8:30 p.m., after a long day of work—gardening, tending chickens, and cooking every single meal (no running to Chipotle if you just don't feel like cooking)—mixed with less daylight and higher altitudes, I'm dropping into bed with a thud. And by the way, I'm sleeping the sleep of the dead, and it's glorious!

But one of the biggest differences I've found living up on the mountain is in how things grow. All the rules I learned about gardening in the city just don't apply here. Everything is harder, takes longer, and is more frustrating.

Predators are a huge problem. When I lived in the suburbs, I would lose my Jesus on the regular, thanks to a neighborhood squirrel that liked to sample my tomatoes and then leave the twice-bitten fruit on the ground. But here on the mountain, the predators come en masse in many shapes and sizes—from a two-pound squirrel to a four-hundred-pound black bear.

In the suburbs, I just had to go to the garden store, grab some pots, dirt, and starter plants, and I was practically guaranteed a salsa garden in a few months, as long as I could keep that one squirrel at bay. But here in the mountains, we spend a lot of time putting up wire cloth, shaving soap (to sprinkle around plants to keep the deer off), and even building a greenhouse just so a few meager plants have a chance of growing.

Between the extreme temperature differences and the forest creatures that think we've planted them their very own Hometown Buffet, we spend the time we used to hang out at Starbucks trying to grow three mostly edible tomatoes. And if the forest-land creatures haven't taken a bite out of them, it's a good day.

Our first year planting things here was a huge exercise in frustration—until my friend Susy, a fellow mountain dweller and experienced gardener, casually dropped a bit of knowledge that restored my faith in God and gardening: "Yeah, it just seems like everything up here takes a lot longer to get going in the garden."

While we had a few blueberries and some amazing cucumbers show up in July and August, it turns out that the rest of our garden is what my mom used to call me when it came to school and studies: a late bloomer. As we rounded the corner into September, we started to see all our hours of planting, feeding, and watering pay off. Dozens of tomatoes hung off the vines like little Christmas tree ornaments. Yellow crooked neck squash exploded like little bursts of sunlight in their wine barrel planters. And the zucchini? Oh, the zucchini! We started looking for unsuspecting neighbors to share it with (that is, dump it on).

But there are advantages to living on the mountain as well. Not the weather, the creatures, or the timing of the seasons. But the resolve you develop. Every time we have a gardening disaster, we get mad, curse the cute deer and bunnies that eat our crop, and then learn what to do better next time. Sure, we've read every book we can get our hands on and done every Google search on how to grow up here on the mountain, but most of the time, our best teacher is failure.

I would not say that one of my best characteristics has ever been perseverance, but up here on the mountain, anything worth doing takes perseverance. It takes the willingness to fail and start again.

Your dreams, and your life, my friend, are worth the perseverance.

I recently had a friend who was so incredibly frustrated with herself over her inability to finish a really important project. She was beating herself up for not finishing and having to start over again. And again.

I didn't have a lot of advice for her, but I did tell her that with each and every failure she experienced, she had to get through it in order to get to the one where she would succeed. Each time she learned something new, chose to grow, and chose to put a little more faith in God than the time before.

Profound? No.

True? For me? Every time.

Your life, your family, your friendships, your dreams, your growth as a child of God? They are all worth doing. And that means they are all worth failing at—over and over again. But after every time you fail, every time you make a mistake, every time you feel that you've disappointed others or God, you are worth growing your resilience and trying it all again.

Growing a garden and growing as a human? They can both be incredibly frustrating, disappointing, and maddening endeavors. And they are both worth doing.

The Next, Most Faith-Filled Step

Is there an area of your life you feel you've given up on?

_____

_____

_____

_____

_____

_____

Take one minute to hand it over to God and ask Him for the next step. Ask God—and wait for the answer—about what the next, most faithful step is. God is persevering for you. You are not alone.

Creating Space

Speak

Read the passage aloud three times.

Ponder

Take a moment to let the words silently flow over you.

Now, some questions to ponder:

What does the passage say?

Why is God bringing you this passage now?

Who comes to mind as you read this passage?

What thoughts come to mind as you ponder?

_____

_____

_____

_____

_____

_____

_____

_____

_____

_____

_____

_____

_____

_____

Act

Is there something God wants you to do because of reading this verse today?

_____

_____

_____

_____

Commit

What has God committed to you in this verse? What promises or truths can you make room for in your thinking?

_____

_____

_____

_____

_____

Express

Finally, take a moment to express aloud to God how you think and feel about your time making space for this piece of Scripture.

_____

_____

_____

_____

_____

A New Normal

CHERI

*Search me, God, and know my heart; test me and
know my anxious thoughts. See if there is any offensive
way in me, and lead me in the way everlasting.*

PSALM 139:23-24

'm scared of your house."

This was the thanks I got for offering Kathi my beach cot-
tage as a writing retreat a year after we moved in.

When I emailed her a short (five pages, typed) list of things
I thought she should know about the house (former army barracks, circa 1940), I expected that as a wordsmith, she'd know the
difference between *quirky* and *scary*.

Take the kitchen, for example:

1. Oven runs HOT. Set it for 50 degrees lower than normal
   unless you enjoy the taste of charcoal. The toaster oven
   burns everything to a crisp. Ditto the electric skillet.
   Microwave, on the other hand, takes fifteen minutes just
   for the little lightbulb inside to go on.
2. Never use more than two plugged-in devices at the same
   time. If you start a third, you'll trip the circuit breaker,

and everything will stop. This means unplugging any charging cell phones if you want to use both the microwave and toaster oven.

3. The refrigerator door fell off last weekend. It generally does this only once every year or two, so we think it's had enough excitement for this year.

I suppose my cautions about the master bathroom might seem a little *different* to someone who hadn't gotten used to the character of the house over several years:

4. Shower temperatures are *opposite* of what you'd expect. So if you're freezing, turn it to the right; scalding, turn it to the left!

5. Scalding isn't likely to be a problem. Water—shower and tap—takes four or five minutes to warm up. You'll hear a change in the tone of the pipes. When the water gets hot, you have exactly ninety seconds before all the hot water is gone until the next day.

6. The window falls out if it's opened more than an inch or two. So far, it's never broken (but there's always a first time!).

Okay, I'll admit, when I reread the list with a more critical eye, some parts did seem kinda scary. Doors and windows that jump out at you, a shower that alternates between freezing and scalding, and kitchen appliances that require you to defend yourself with a fire extinguisher weren't exactly normal.

As I made a new list—a fix-it list intended to lower the number of "quirks" in the house—I wondered how much poor treatment I willingly accept from other people, assuring myself, "It's not scary; it's normal!"

And how much of my own bad behavior do I excuse by saying, "I'm a bit quirky! It's just my character!" Who am I scalding with my frustration flares while at the same time reassuring myself, *They should be used to my hot-and-cold habits by now?* What relationships are turning crispy when I unexpectedly overheat in anger, even as I let myself off the hook because *They should know better than to push my buttons?*

Just as I handed my fix-it list to my landlord, I also need to turn over my personal "quirk" list to the Holy Spirit. Some of what I consider normal really is pretty scary, after all. But I know from God's Word and years of personal experience that He is faithful to do far more than just a quick fix. God specializes in transformation.

Sure, we can stick to our "It's normal" story and allow our so-called quirks to keep hurting the people we love. Or we can attempt to overhaul our character defects on our own.

It's so much better to hand our struggles over to God.

Like David, we too can approach God with vulnerability and transparency and pray Psalm 139:23-24: "Search me, God, and know my heart; test me and know my anxious thoughts. See if there is any offensive way in me, and lead me in the way everlasting."

We can connect with Jesus throughout each day via Scripture and prayer. We can remind ourselves that only through Jesus, our Savior, will true change take place. We need Jesus, our Savior! The more we get to know Him, the more our relationship with Him will grow. We will depend on Him more and be increasingly "transformed into his image" (2 Corinthians 3:18).

And we can seek wise counsel to support us through the growth process. A spiritual mentor or Christian counselor can cut quickly to core issues, provide loving accountability, and help us hear the still small voice of God speaking to our hearts.

Just as an old house doesn't become "scary" overnight, your character "quirks" have developed from years of repetition and reinforcement. When we depend on God's transformative process in our lives, when we surrender our list to Him, He may change some things immediately, miraculously. Or He may, as it seems is more often the case, transform us over time, allowing circumstances in our lives that offer opportunities for growth.

Opportunities to become more and more like Him.

The Next, Most Faith-Filled Step

Prayerfully process—or pray-cess—these questions:

What scary "quirks" do others expect me to tolerate in them?

_____

_____

_____

What scary "quirks" have I been expecting others to tolerate in me?

_____

_____

_____

Creating Space

Speak

Read the passage aloud three times.

Ponder

Take a moment to let the words silently flow over you.

Now, some questions to ponder:

What does the passage say?

Why is God bringing you this passage now?

Who comes to mind as you read this passage?

What thoughts come to mind as you ponder?

_____

_____

_____

_____

_____

_____

_____

_____

_____

_____

_____

_____

_____

_____

Act

Is there something God wants you to do because of reading this verse today?

_____

_____

_____

_____

Commit

What has God committed to you in this verse? What promises or truths can you make room for in your thinking?

_____

_____

_____

_____

_____

Express

Finally, take a moment to express aloud to God how you think and feel about your time making space for this piece of Scripture.

_____

_____

_____

_____

_____

Checking Myself into the Greenhouse

KATHI

The apostles gathered around Jesus and reported to him all they had done and taught. Then, because so many people were coming and going that they did not even have a chance to eat, he said to them, "Come with me by yourselves to a quiet place and get some rest."

MARK 6:30-31

This summer, I mentioned to my husband that I thought I would really like a greenhouse. We had been working on our garden a lot, but I knew that fall and winter were coming, and all that beautiful squash, zucchini, and tomatoes (oh, the tomatoes!) would be a distant memory. (And once you've had the deep, complex taste of a homegrown tomato, it's very hard to go back to the watery red orbs that most supermarkets offer.)

So with an abundance of time, and plans off the Internet, my engineering husband became Bob the Builder and built me a greenhouse that's the envy of the forest animals. (Because of COVID, they are the only ones who have actually seen the greenhouse.)

One of my favorite features of the greenhouse is the design for the different stages of our plants. On the shelf in the back of the greenhouse are our seedlings. These are the shallow trays I started in our kitchen with seeds from those little packages you get from Home Depot or order from the seed catalog.

When they start to sprout, the seedlings graduate to the back of the greenhouse to get heartier. It's so fun to watch the miracle that are seeds sprouting in your kitchen, knowing they will eventually return to your kitchen to become that wonderful salad or baked zucchini. These are the plants that get babied by me and my husband. They're the first ones I check to see if they're still thriving. We water them so, so carefully; we check the pH balance regularly.

On the right shelf of the greenhouse are our plants that have made it through the delicate stage of sprouting. We take the strongest seedlings and plant them in the larger trays on the right side of the house in the soil, so they can really establish roots and grow strong. We plant tons of seedlings to see which will grow the strongest and have the best chance of surviving. (Come to think of it, our garden is a little bit like *The Hunger Games*. Plants that are the strongest move on to the next stage of planting. "And may the odds be ever in your favor, little crooked-neck squash!")

When some of our garden plants, those outside the greenhouse, aren't doing well—maybe they've missed a watering cycle, or they just need some extra love and attention—I tell them it's okay. "You just need some time in the greenhouse."

Once in the greenhouse, we can pay extra special attention to the plant. We'll analyze the soil content and the water levels and, well, just baby the plant until we can find out why it's not thriving.

I've noticed over the past year or so, when circumstances have really knocked me off my feet and people's opinions of me and those I love have been less than flattering, or even when I've done great things but find myself exhausted, I need a little extra love, protection, and nurturing in order to recover. I need extra time to heal and grow. To be kept safe from predators, to be taken care of in a way that promotes healing and growth.

In other words, at my lowest, I sometimes need to check myself into the greenhouse.

I love what Jesus does in Mark 6. The apostles gathered around Jesus and reported to Him all they had done and taught. "Then, because so many people were coming and going that they did not even have a chance to eat, he said to them, 'Come with me by yourselves to a quiet place and get some rest'" (verse 31).

The disciples were so excited to tell Jesus about all the things they had accomplished. Jesus's response? "You look like you could use a good lunch and a bit of a lie down." Jesus was less concerned about what they had done and more concerned about how they were doing. He understood the concept of taking time away from accomplishing great things in order to rest and restore, so that the Father can do great things for us, body and spirit.

What does checking myself into the greenhouse actually look like? It might look like this:

A *social media sabbatical.* Sometimes I need to stay away from others' thoughtless words (or the well-thought-out words that are intended to inflict harm). This is especially true when there's a scandal breaking or any time there's an election.

Curating my friends. This is a controversial one for sure. But just as I'm careful about who I bring into my home, I'm now incredibly careful about who I bring in (or let stay) in my social media life. People forget themselves online, and just like I spend a lot of time deciding what I let into my greenhouse (Bees? Good. Squirrels? Bad.), I must be careful to only let people into my life whom God has assigned me to be in relationship with or are good for my soul.

Getting the good stuff into me. When I'm in the greenhouse, I'm super intentional about all those habits that can be challenging to maintain while interacting with the real world. This is the time I double down on praying, reading the Bible, and listening to worship music. These are simple things, but it's amazing how often, when I'm not in a healthy place, it's easy to skip the things that bring me life.

Growth and restoration happen in the greenhouse. It looks different, but sometimes it's necessary in order to protect our mind and our heart—so we can be strong enough when the time comes to brave the elements.

The Next, Most Faith-Filled Step

What are your signs that it's time to check yourself into the greenhouse? For me, it's when I stop doing all the things that are nurturing for myself, and for those I love. When I'm staying up too late. When I'm eating things that aren't healthy and don't even taste that great—like cheap chocolate. When I have time to watch TV reruns, but not have a conversation with a friend.

Write down your own signs here so the next time they are happening, you can notice the signs and take some time to pull back, spend some time with Jesus, and get healthy.

_____

_____

_____

_____

_____

_____

_____

_____

Creating Space

Speak

Read the passage aloud three times.

Ponder

Take a moment to let the words silently flow over you.

Now, some questions to ponder:

What does the passage say?

Why is God bringing you this passage now?

Who comes to mind as you read this passage?

What thoughts come to mind as you ponder?

_____

_____

_____

_____

_____

_____

_____

_____

_____

_____

_____

_____

Act

Is there something God wants you to do because of reading this verse today?

_____

_____

_____

_____

Commit

What has God committed to you in this verse? What promises or truths can you make room for in your thinking?

_____

_____

_____

_____

_____

Express

Finally, take a moment to express aloud to God how you think and feel about your time making space for this piece of Scripture.

_____

_____

_____

_____

_____

Right Where You Are Right Now

CHERI

*All my longings lie open before you, Lord; my sighing
is not hidden from you. My heart pounds, my strength
fails me; even the light has gone from my eyes. . . . LORD,
do not forsake me; do not be far from me, my God.
Come quickly to help me, my Lord and my Savior.*

PSALM 38:9-10, 21-22

The phone rings.

I reach to answer, but then caller ID flashes on the screen. My hand hovers as two competing needs play tug-of-war within me. One is the need to remain loyal, to conform to habit, to simply pick up the phone and say, "Hey there! How are you?" The other is a newer need, one that's been growing at a surprising pace: the need to quit faking fine.

The phone rings again, and I teeter between duty and desire. I know the person calling loves me. I also know that our conversation will follow one of two scripts.

In the first, when they ask, "How are you?" I will muster up my best acting skills and put on a convincing performance. And they will be thrilled, *thrilled* to hear I'm doing so well. They will praise God that their prayers for me are being answered. They will affirm me for doing all the right things: reading my Bible, praying, keeping a gratitude journal, serving others.

In the second script, when they ask, "How are you?" I will tell the truth. I am doing all the right things: reading my Bible, praying, keeping a gratitude journal, serving others. And I am exhausted. Depleted. Discouraged. Possibly depressed. After a brief pause—during which it will be deafeningly obvious that they will not be praising God that their prayers for me are being answered—they will muster up a pick-me-up speech meant to fix me.

I will do my best to listen while simultaneously choking back tears. I will know they want to help, but I will feel an undercurrent of blame for not trying hard enough to hold myself together. And I will feel dismissed, as if their need for positivity is a higher priority than my current reality.

I'm in a season of unremitting grief, feeling a cascade of losses in very vivid ways.

Well-meaning friends and family members keep telling me about specific practices they're leaning into that make them feel much more upbeat and positive. I'm not questioning them; I believe them. Whenever they tell me about their helpful habits, I feel pressure to come up with my own go-to solution so I can sound equally positive.

But the truth is, sometimes lament is the right response to

seasons of grief. Like a coastal fog that shrouds the sun and surrounding terrain, when grief descends, what was once positive and light becomes burdensome, and our souls become unnavigable. It is then we lament . . .

> All my longings lie open before you, Lord;
>   my sighing is not hidden from you.
> My heart pounds, my strength fails me;
>   even the light has gone from my eyes.

Desperate, we cry out to God . . .

> LORD, do not forsake me;
>   do not be far from me, my God.
> Come quickly to help me,
>   my Lord and my Savior.

We trust that the sun will break through the fog, the season will shift, and sunlight will glisten on the bay once again.

Although I crave human understanding, I know I cannot expect from humans what only God can provide. So instead, I follow David's lead and call out to the One who can handle my sorrow.

Letting the phone call go to voicemail, I sit down in my prayer chair with my Bible and prayer journal. There, I pour out my heart and my tears to God with no restraint. I'll return the call when I'm not a ticking time bomb of reactivity, ready to detonate on an unsuspecting friend or family member. First, I need to be real and raw with God alone.

It's okay to feel a deep sense of loss with God. It's such a relief to know He sees us where we actually are. Not where others wish us to be, expect us to be, need us to be. God can handle every single bit of our humanity. With Him, there's no dismissiveness, no reprimand, no round-about hinting about how you should be feeling. No cliché, "Pain is inevitable, but misery is optional!"

With God, you never ever need to fake fine. You are seen by God. You are known by God. You are loved by God. Right where you are, right now.

The Next, Most Faith-Filled Step

Make room for lament in your life. Go to God with your grief and confusion; be honest about your complaint. Ask for His deliverance and trust that He will show up.

Go to God.

Be honest.

Ask for deliverance.

Trust Him.

Creating Space

Speak

Read the passage aloud three times.

Ponder

Take a moment to let the words silently flow over you.

Now, some questions to ponder:

    What does the passage say?

    Why is God bringing you this passage now?

    Who comes to mind as you read this passage?

    What thoughts come to mind as you ponder?

_____

_____

_____

_____

_____

_____

_____

_____

_____

_____

_____

_____

Act

Is there something God wants you to do because of reading this verse today?

_____

_____

_____

_____

Commit

What has God committed to you in this verse? What promises or truths can you make room for in your thinking?

_____

_____

_____

_____

_____

Express

Finally, take a moment to express aloud to God how you think and feel about your time making space for this piece of Scripture.

_____

_____

_____

_____

_____

Hope in a Seed Catalog

KATHI

Praise be to the God and Father of our Lord Jesus Christ!
In his great mercy he has given us new birth into a
living hope through the resurrection of Jesus Christ
from the dead, and into an inheritance
that can never perish, spoil or fade.

1 PETER 1:3-4

I've always dreamed of having a large, luscious garden—one I'd go to in the morning (long white gauzy dress optional) to pick fresh berries for breakfast and cut flowers to put on our long kitchen table.

When we moved to the mountain, I imagined myself sitting on our porch on spring afternoons, sipping iced tea while leafing through seed catalogs.

Adorable, but not at all realistic.

Instead, because a garden requires planning ahead, the reality is that during the winter, I'm curled up on our couch with a steaming cup of dark coffee and a seed catalog. I wait for our ancient fireplace to heat up the room while the cat and dog jockey for a position on my lap as I try to turn the pages over their heads.

Ordering seeds in January is a radical act of hope. In January, you've already been stuck on the mountain a couple of times because of an "unusual" snowstorm, the weather has lost its charm, and the thought of anything growing under the currently frozen earth seems as likely as escaping our snowed-in house by flying out on a unicorn.

But to have a garden in the summer, you must be willing to dare to dream in the winter.

A beautiful summer garden requires imagination and hope in the dark and dreary months of December and January. So even though it seems impossible and a bit silly to be picking out what variety of squash you'll be serving at the dinner table in July, we gardeners grab our notepads and start making lists of the flowers, berries, herbs, and veggies we want to be surrounded with during the summer.

This winter, I'm finally picking up my catalog again after abandoning it for over a month due to the illness and, sadly, the passing of my mother-in-law, Betty. And isn't timing such an interesting thing? Typically, a month ago, I would have normally been dreaming about all the beautiful flowers and luscious vegetables I could look forward to in the heat of late summer. But now, my thoughts turn to the hope of our garden and the hope that Betty had in life.

Betty loved her three boys, including my husband, Roger, her youngest. And while she expressed that love, it was always with longing for the people she loved who had already passed — her sister, Helen, her lifelong best friend, as well as her husband, Dean, who had preceded her in death by about eight years. While Betty loved her boys on this side of heaven, she never stopped longing to be with Jesus and reunited with those she loved. She was able to enjoy her boys and the lives they'd built and, at the same time, keep an eye on heaven, where her hope lay.

For so long, I've feared change. I want things to stay the same because, in the past, change has meant loss. And in each season up here on the mountain, there is loss. But there is also, always, something to look forward to.

In winter, we lose so much of the life and color, but we gain rest (far fewer chores to do in the winter), time together as a couple, and the antics of Moose the dog rediscovering her inner snow bunny as she scampers through the forest, leaving snowy pawprints in her wake.

In the spring, we lose the snow and long days of snuggling by the fire, but we gain the first signs of new life.

As summer approaches, we lose the cool afternoons that the mountain is made for, being outside all day long. But in the summer, the berries and vegetables start to really put on a show. The tomatoes beg to be pulled off the vine, the basil plant hanging heavy with leaves gets picked, and both get paired with homemade mozzarella, olive oil, and salt. Add homemade bread and we have our perfect summer lunch.

As fall presents itself, we start to lose the long, star-filled evenings around the fire and instead, enjoy the bite in the air that says, "Start the fire, but bring a blanket."

There are losses each season.

There is beauty each season.

There is hope for each new season.

This winter, I'm looking at seed catalogs with a new kind of hope. Betty was also known for her love of all things butterflies. Roger said when you didn't know what to get his mom for Christmas or her birthday, get her something with a butterfly. It would always bring her a smile.

As I've done more research about butterflies, I can see why Betty loved them so much. Butterflies are a sign of hope. Hope of change. Hope of new life. Hope of something better to come.

So this year, as I pour through the seed catalogs, I'm looking with purpose. I'm ordering the lilacs and milkweeds, marigolds and zinnias. These are the plants known in my area to attract butterflies. We're taking a portion of our mountain and creating a butterfly garden. Dedicated to Betty. Dedicated to hope.

Why a garden dedicated to hope? Because like ordering seeds in January, sometimes our day-to-day life here on earth requires a big dose of radical hope. The hope of new life. The hope of something better to come in the days ahead. The hope of eternity spent with Jesus.

Daily, we need to remind ourselves of that hope. And a garden, no matter if it's on the page, a seed, growing, or withering? All of those stages are a reminder of hope.

The Next, Most Faith-Filled Step

What is the tangible dose of hope you need to remember that God has something good in store?

_____

_____

_____

_____

_____

_____

_____

_____

For me, it's the butterfly garden. For you, it might be a Bible verse tacked up above your computer monitor or a picture of nature on the windowsill of your kitchen.

Go find and display that piece of tangible hope right now to remind you of your living hope.

Creating Space

Speak

Read the passage aloud three times.

Ponder

Take a moment to let the words silently flow over you.

Now, some questions to ponder:

What does the passage say?

Why is God bringing you this passage now?

Who comes to mind as you read this passage?

What thoughts come to mind as you ponder?

_____

_____

_____

_____

_____

_____

_____

_____

_____

_____

_____

_____

_____

Act

Is there something God wants you to do because of reading this verse today?

_____

_____

_____

_____

Commit

What has God committed to you in this verse? What promises or truths can you make room for in your thinking?

_____

_____

_____

_____

_____

Express

Finally, take a moment to express aloud to God how you think and feel about your time making space for this piece of Scripture.

_____

_____

_____

_____

_____

About the Authors

With wisdom and humor, **Kathi Lipp** offers hope paired with practical steps to live with meaning. Kathi is the author of 20 books, including *Clutter Free*, *The Christmas Project Planner*, *The Get Yourself Organized Project*, *The Husband Project*, and *Overwhelmed*. She is the host of the Clutter Free Academy Podcast and speaks at conferences across the country. She is often featured on Woman's World as one of their "Ask the Experts," Focus on the Family, MOPS International, Crosswalk.com, Girlfriends in God, and on Proverbs 31 Ministries, where she is part of the (in)Courage team of writers for Dayspring. Follow her on Instagram @kathilipp.

Through Scripture and storytelling, **Cheri Gregory** delights in helping women draw closer to Jesus, the strength of every tender heart. She is the coleader of Sensitive and Strong: the place for the HSP Christian woman to find connection; the cohost, with Amy Carroll, of *Grit 'n' Grace—the Podcast*; the founder of Write Beside You communicator coaching; and the coauthor, with Kathi Lipp, of *You Don't Have to Try So Hard* and *Overwhelmed*. Cheri speaks locally and internationally for women's events and educational conferences. She and her college sweetheart, Daniel, have been married for more than three decades. They've spent the last 15 years living and serving on the campus of Monterey Bay Academy on the central California coast.

To learn more about Harvest House books and
to read sample chapters, visit our website:

www.harvesthousepublishers.com

HARVEST HOUSE PUBLISHERS
EUGENE, OREGON